T0365135

Principals

Nancy Love, PhD,
Mel Blitzer,
Marjorie Munroe

PIINC

Suite 640, 1300, 8th Street SW
Calgary AB
T2R 1B2
www.pulseinstitute.com

Order this book online at www.trafford.com
or email orders@trafford.com

Most Trafford titles are also available at major online book retailers.

Printed in Victoria, BC, Canada.

ISBN: 978-1-4269-2797-3 (sc)
ISBN: 978-1-4269-2799-7 (eb)

Library of Congress Control Number: 2010902469

Our mission is to efficiently provide the world's finest, most comprehensive book publishing service, enabling every author to experience success. To find out how to publish your book, your way, and have it available worldwide, visit us online at www.trafford.com

Trafford rev. 4/13/2010

 www.trafford.com

North America & international
toll-free: 1 888 232 4444 (USA & Canada)
phone: 250 383 6864 ✦ fax: 812 355 4082

Contents

Chapter 1: Accountability and Change — 1

Chapter 2: The Impresario — 11

Chapter 3: The Sherpa — 33

Chapter 4: The Coach — 48

Chapter 5: The Rescuer — 65

Chapter 6: The Gardener — 81

Chapter 7: A Call to Action — 100

Epilogue: The Voice of a Principal — 109

Acknowledgements — 111

About the Authors — 112

Reading List — 114

Chapter 1: Accountability and Change

As a principal you know that there are many different routes to success. And no doubt you have had your fair share of discussions about measures of success in a school. This book will introduce you to five principals who have their own stories to tell about managing a mandated change. Through them you will discover, compare and contrast a variety of approaches to responding to change and managing transitions.

Perhaps you will find yourself or a colleague reflected here, and gain insight into how your actions are perceived and received. Or perhaps you are facing a significant change yourself, and will gather inspiration from the narratives of others. Either way, you will be intrigued and perhaps surprised by these real-life stories. In researching her PhD dissertation, and while conducting research for this book, Nancy Love interviewed five high school principals in a Canadian province. The principals work in both Catholic and public school jurisdictions, and their schools range from a small community school in a resort town to a large junior and senior high in a suburban community. Names and details have been changed to preserve anonymity, but the circumstances have not.

The Principals

You will meet Paul Markum, the Impresario. Paul is a gregarious, charismatic fellow. He is a revered leader who has worked in many settings including elementary, middle and high schools. For Paul Markum education is the show. He is convinced that teachers need to focus on teaching future actors in life, not merely presenting the scripts which we call curriculum. He holds strong opinions, often uses strong language and will do whatever he can to give students a chance at education, thus preparing them to step onto life's stage in whatever roles they have chosen. Markum serves many roles in his school: producer, director, improviser, ensuring that the show *will* go on despite the changes that challenge his vision.

You will read the story of Ted Norquay, the Sherpa. Ted shoulders a lot of draining administrative work, enabling his staff to focus more clearly on teaching students. He is a guide carrying an immense load in a school that saw the greatest increase in test scores. He protects his fellow climbers from the burden of paper work and supervision as he guides them to the summit. The teachers are not aware of all Ted does for them as he quietly shoulders more and more work in the ever-thinning air. He does not seek gratitude. Like a Sherpa, he climbs toward the summit, unrelenting and under great weight with no way to share his burdens with those he serves.

Rich O'Sullivan is the Coach of coaches. He places critical importance on test scores and measurable performance. He runs a school with small class sizes in a small, remote locale where teachers are held to high account by parents and members of the community. The emphasis in the school is on achievement. However, sport is important as well as results in the classroom. Rich does whatever he can to ensure his teacher-coaches have the training needed to get their teams ready for the contest; the mandated exams. He gives his teachers the experience they need by sending them to be exam markers and by encouraging field testing. In this way he influences teachers to take exam writing seriously. This Coach knows the game and the rules. He works with the talent on his team to perform.

The Rescuer is William Johnson, a highly experienced high school principal with a physical education background. His Catholic high school serves both junior and high school students. He has been hired to fly in and rescue a school that is in trouble, with high staff turnover and reported dysfunction. Johnson has done it before. He has come to the rescue of staff and students in other schools, and he is ready to do so again. Johnson knows the community and he is confident in his own ability to show them the way out of the mess they are in. His mission is clear: rescue the school.

And finally you will meet the Gardener, Matthew Hunter, who gently nurtures his students to grow towards success. The garden is well organized and purposeful. Deliberate steps have been taken since the beginning to ensure the right balance of nurturing and self-discipline for students to grow to their full potential. He has organized his new school into "colleges" to create smaller schools within a bigger institution, and he is using teacher advisor groups to create a sense of belonging and community in the school. He wants all students to receive the attention they require to get to graduation. He supports the teachers, students, parents and the structure of the school through an emphasis on independent and mastery learning. Individualization of programs and opportunities is important to him. Matthew believes this focus will allow each plot and plant to contribute as individuals to the long-term unfolding of a successful garden.

Working with This Book

The purpose of introducing you to these principals and their stories is to incite dialogue around how to respond to mandated change. The portraits of the five principals in the study are "drawn" from an appreciative use of metaphors, a tool often used in the education of leaders. The metaphors serve to illustrate five different approaches to managing the transitions that result from imposed change. The intention is that other principals and educational administrators will learn from the experiences of those portrayed here and apply the lessons in their own work and to their own realities.

The portraits of The Gardner, The Rescuer, The Impresario, The Sherpa and The Coach are presented in Chapters 2 through 6. Some guiding questions for applying the lessons to real-life situations can be found in Chapter 7. What will you do with the things you have learned?

Leaders of Change in School

The principals profiled in this book were chosen because they successfully responded to changes in policy at the jurisdictional level around accountability in schools. Similar changes were being made in many countries around the world with the intent of ensuring public accountability for student progress in schools. The measure of student achievement is based on marks attained on standardized tests. These principals approached the implementation of the new policies and practices for accountability in different ways. This book considers the connection between practices of principals (what they did) and improved student outcomes (the test scores). How do principals influence the situation in the classroom from the school office?

These five principals were required to implement three significant changes:

1. To adjust to receiving funding based on the number of high school credits their student populations complete.

2. To write annual three-year business plans for their schools with measurable outcomes aligned with jurisdiction and district goals.

3. To prepare annual school reports for the jurisdiction and the public that reflect progress on the goals outlined in the business plans.

These portraits are an outsider's appreciative interpretation of what happened as a result of the mandated change and of how successful transitions were made in response to the new policies. The portraits provide an opportunity to learn about the impact of mandated change and how each principal, in his own way, mitigated the effects of implementing the new policies.

The portraits are based on real situations, settings and identities. Though masked to maintain confidentiality, the situations remain essentially true and are common enough that readers may recognize what seems to be a familiar set of circumstances, no matter the time or place. There are lessons to be learned. How do you get people to "buy into" or accept a mandated change? What tools can you use to assure staff and parents of the wisdom of the change? How can you motivate staff to accept responsibility or hold them accountable for the necessary changes in behaviour and the organizational and personal transitions that must occur for success?

Transitions in Accountability

The transition these principals were leading was a common one. A shift in accountability for student results began in the 1980s and continued after *Better Schools* was published in Britain and *A Nation at Risk* was published in the United States. School jurisdictions, principals and head masters all around the world were held to public account for the standardized test results of their charges. An example of the kind of documents that were being produced at the time follows:

Principles in Accountability (Accountability in Education: Policy Framework 1995)

1. Provincially mandated goals, strategies and measures for school boards and schools

2. Additional goals, strategies and measures to reflect local needs

3. The development, by school boards, of policies and processes for schools to address school planning and reporting

4. The determination by schools, in accordance with board policy, of additional goals, strategies and measures to reflect local needs, and to be responsive to advice from the school council

5. The phase-in of provincially mandated reporting requirements for school boards in which student achievement, student programs and financial information are reported

6. The involvement of school councils as key participants

7. Provincial Education reports on the performance of the department

The Shift in the Principal's Role

Concern about the performance of schools has mounted, while at the same time there is an appreciation of the complexity of school reform. When systems are complex, and when the tendencies of such systems are toward overload and fragmentation, the need for leadership to forge synergy and coherence is paramount. The increased emphasis on accountability and business planning has created a more entrepreneurial role for the principal as he seeks to fund his school by attracting students to new and exciting programs or providing better opportunities than the school down the road. All of this change was magnified by the massive budget cutting that accompanied the increase in responsibility. The result has been role ambiguity of massive proportions for school principals and a role overload that has made the job much more difficult than expected.

I was a High School Principal

I became a high school principal as result of an article I wrote as a vice principal lamenting the effects of a budget cutback that was published in a local newsletter. My superintendent at the time decided I was no longer fit for school administration and after a tirade of about forty-five minutes pronounced that he could no longer protect me. I was summarily assigned back to the classroom. That was not how I saw things. I liked administration so I applied elsewhere. The "elsewhere" I was offered was a position as principal of a small high school. I took up the challenge.

At my first meeting with the superintendent of the district our conversation went something like this. I had some questions. "When would I meet my Vice Principal?"

"Well," he said, "she is out of province. Her mother is very sick and I'm not sure she'll be back much before school begins. By the way she has asked to be transferred to another school but I haven't answered her request ... yet."

I paused, a little taken aback and wondering what it would be like to be in a new town at a new school with no continuity in the administrative team. "What about the secretarial staff?"

"Well," he said, "the secretary was married to one of our board members and the board went on a retreat and there was this 'Payton Place' kind of thing that happened so she has left town.... There is a part time secretary. She's delightful but she doesn't know anything about the student records system." My eyebrows moved a centimetre higher.

"What about the counsellor?"

"Well," he said, "you have been assigned a new counsellor. Last year's counsellor was the Phys Ed guy. He isn't looking forward to going back to the gym but we have this psychologist who used to be in central office who needed the position. He commutes 5 hours every weekend so he probably won't be here until just before school starts. We have a counsellor coming back off deferred salary leave but we are putting her into the behavioural needs program. She hasn't done that before so you'll have to let her go to visit some other programs before we get ours really up and running. We are having a ministerial review on the new program she will be implementing in January or February, so we need to get it right. We're fighting some bad publicity on that one so it has to be a Cracker Jack program. She and her husband were on deferred salary leave last year. Her husband has been placed at the middle school. You might know him. He was the principal here before they left."

Oh great I thought. What next? "What about the Community School Program?"

"Well," he said, "As you know the funding has been cut. I need you to make sure we squeeze enough money out of this *budget to maintain the half-time coordinator. She is great and should retire soon."*

Hmmmm. "What about the community library?"

"Well," he said, "the school librarian and the municipal librarian hate each other.... They have sort of drawn a line with masking tape down the middle of the library space. We are hoping that with your background in libraries that you will be able to get that library working the way it should."

Okay, I thought, add it to my list of miracles. "When will the teachers be back?"

"Well," he said, "I wanted to talk to you about that. We had this Teacher's Association thing and I'm not sure how it was left. Teachers were asking for some independence on the organizational days and hinting that they might stay home to get organized... so if they don't show up on the 27th be sure and let me know. By the way," he added, "the students were quite fond of the old principal. They demonstrated when we let him go. They chained themselves to the door. We had the media in and everything. I think they are over that now. And you should probably keep an eye on the caretaking staff. These ladies have been doing this work for years. This year we went to contracts so they formed their own company and made a bid. I'm not sure how it is going to work out."

Of course, I thought. Not even the custodial work will be simple. "We have great parents in this community," the super continued "... a little rebellious at times. So far they have refused to form a school council...."

As I left the meeting with the Super, I found my thoughts racing in chaotic concert with my emotions, but soon convinced myself that the reality of the current school situation could not be as bad as I imagined. Once I actually entered the school, life would be challenging but I would manage from a place of centeredness and logic as I always had in the past.

My first day in the building, I arrived early. It had been raining hard all night but had cleared to a glorious sunny August morning. I was met at the door by a man who said, "You don't want to go in there."

"I'm the new principal."

"I know who you are and you don't want to go in there." Reluctantly he led me in and showed me the newly painted and carpeted office that would be mine now splattered with tar from the hole in the roof that had been covered by a tarp the night before awaiting the new overhead heating unit that would arrive today. "We'll have to do it all again," he said as he showed me to my temporary quarters across the hall in the small Community School Office cramped with four desks where one used to sit comfortably. Shortly after I had set up camp I met my first teacher. I greeted him warmly apologizing for not having found the master schedule by then so that I could provide him with a timetable he was requesting.

"Well," he said, "if there are computer courses on it I'm going to grieve it!"

That was the beginning, a shock orientation to a new reality for which I felt ill prepared. Later that year the small district that hired me was amalgamated with a bigger district and the few supports we had from the central office, including the superintendent who had put his faith in me, were gone overnight. Budget concerns loomed large and uncertainty was everywhere. Many times thoughts of running away crossed my mind but eventually one by one I was able to build the relationships that resulted in a well functioning school. Over the course of the following years, managing and leading as principal, I always wondered whether there was a better way to prepare leaders and the staff they serve for change and the inevitable very human, often messy transitions that follow.

Dr. Nancy Love, Author

Our hope here is that principals and other school leaders read these stories and adapt the lessons learned from the experience of their colleagues. Since Wolcott wrote *The Man in the Principal's Office* in the 1970s we have been fascinated with the way decisions are made by individuals in that office. Yet there are few volumes that describe the different responses to mandated change. Each jurisdiction and each district, in fact each school, interprets what needs to be done differently for successful implementation. Knowing that there is "no one way" is liberating. Now let's look at the portraits to see just how different, and effective, the responses can be. You will notice at the end of each chapter a summary of the characteristics of each principal, along with thoughts on what they need to work effectively, and what followers need to know to work effectively with them.

Chapter 2: The Impresario

Rosedale Composite High School

It's the greatest show on earth!
On with the show!

The audience is largely unaware of the work of the Impresario, but without him there would be no show. Behind the scenes he acts as producer, promoter, financier, maestro and politician, standing large, front and centre in pulling together the big show. He knows his audience and knows the resources he requires. He knows the actors he needs to deliver the very best performance. He cajoles, he charms, he pushes, he connects, he talks, he walks, he tames the doubting tiger, he balances on the high wire above the stakeholders, and at the right moment, he flies through the air with the greatest of ease.

The neighbourhood surrounding Rosedale has grown significantly since it was built in the 1980s. At that time, although it remained inside the city limits of St. Anne and served the population of the growing city, it was situated in a farmer's field on the edge of town. The city has grown to meet it over the past decade. New expensive homes fill the once rural setting. The neighbourhood has changed and so has the population of the school. The affluent, suburban city of St. Anne is home to four high schools; two are in the Catholic Board. There is little industry in St. Anne. It is a bedroom community with activities and facilities for families, restaurants and retail.

Rosedale provides a composite program focusing on academics and trades, and it is well equipped for occupational education.

The other local high school has been in operation for more than 35 years and has a strong reputation for academics. Although it is situated on the other side of town, and geography and access to transportation play a role in their choices, students are free to choose the school they will attend. The community had known the schools were different for a long time. The one was steeped in academic tradition and the other, Rosedale, was rough and catered to non-academics.

Rosedale has fought hard to gain a reputation as both an academic and a non-academic school. Under the watchful eye of principal Paul Markum, Rosedale has developed a new sense of PRIDE; in fact, the web site proudly boasts this school motto:

Politeness,

Respect for yourself, others and property,

Integrity,

Dignity, and

Excellence.

Markum promotes Rosedale as the "Greatest academic and non-academic show on earth". He is the Impresario and education is the show at Rosedale.

The Impresario

Paul Markum is a big man, 6 foot 4 inches tall. As a Junior High School Math and French teacher in the late 1970s, students loved him. They showed him a respect that came from his size and his presence, and from the size of his heart, which is proportionately large. Paul cares about students. He does anything for them—he wants all of them to succeed. His dedication to students has never faded throughout his career. Students want to be successful with him, and so do teachers. Paul Markum, as principal of Rosedale Composite, has created a school with a good story to tell about how to make a difference for students. He is still the big guy with the big heart who expects students to behave and to get their work done. What is different now is that he expects things of teachers and other staff members. He seems to be experiencing the same respect from the teachers and staff that he earned as a teacher in the early years with students. Rosedale Composite achieved increases in average test scores for three years running, an accomplishment worthy of recognition. This is a story about *The Impresario*, and the leadership practices that have contributed to increased test scores.

Defining the Roles

To Paul it is pretty basic: "Something I have learned working through elementary, junior high and senior high is that you have to teach students not curriculum." For years at junior high Paul preached that teachers at that level should teach students. He

> "Something I have learned working through elementary, junior high school and senior high is that you have to teach students not curriculum."
>
> Paul Markum, Impresario

believed that high school would take care of curriculum. When he came to high school, he found that was exactly what was happening. Teachers were teaching curriculum. "When I first arrived here I walked around with my master key in my hand all the time. If I wanted to go in a classroom I would have to unlock the door in maybe half the classrooms." The problem here for Paul was that the teachers were locking doors and locking students out of the classroom. He was curious about where the students were if they were not in the classrooms. He discovered that the cafeteria was full.

In the cafeteria there were cards at every table, and there were circles of 40 to 60 students at any given time playing hacky sack. Students who arrived late for class were locked out, so they went out and played hacky sack or they played cards. They did not go to class. Markum explained that they did not go to class because they were not invited. They did not go to class because the doors were locked. Instead of fighting with the teacher to get in, they would go outside and play hacky sack.

> I would walk outside and say, "Hello, what is going on here?" They would say, "Do you want to join us?" I would tell them that what I wanted was for them to go to class. The students

would mention the locked doors to me and I would say, "Just come with me and I will open it," and I did.

Markum arrived at Rosedale in a cold January ten years ago. By May, he was ready to move. His commitment to treating each student as an individual and doing what is best for the student in each instance was being challenged in this environment. "It was a tough go. It was a really tough go." His vice-principal was a man he had worked with before. Their roles had been reversed at an elementary school where the vice-principal had served as principal and Markum had served as vice-principal. Markum used to call this man the consummate principal: a person who did everything around students and community. He had taught Markum how to bring the community into the school. At Rosedale, as vice-principal, Markum's colleague was a different person—an angry, wizened old man. "I just looked at him and thought, 'What happened?'" Whatever it was, Markum was determined not to let it happen to him.

Markum spent very little time in the office initially. He was always in the hallway. He walked and he walked, and he talked to the students. He opened classroom doors, and he went into every classroom in the school. Everything would stop when he entered. Teachers and students wondered what he wanted. "I do not want anything, I am just cruising," he would say. About a year and a half later they began to understand that Markum cruises. Some of the people who were at Rosedale eight and a half years ago are still there. Many have retired or moved on. There are also many new teachers hired by Markum with the understanding that they will teach students not curriculum. "... the kid is the most important part of this building."

Audience and Participation

Markum does not believe that giving ownership to the students means that teachers and staff give up any authority. "Have we turned the asylum over to the inmates? Not in the least." Markum believes that the staff works hard to develop feelings of ownership among students. He reports that the students feel that they are capable of running the school because the staff provides the opportunities for them to be involved. Activities that happen at the school happen because of the students, not because of the teachers. The staff provides the mentors. They are the "support". Markum describes them as supporting rather than managing the student activities. When there is an open house, for example, the students do the planning and organizing. The students tell the staff what they think the junior high students might want to see. They tell the staff how they want to do it and they ask teachers for help. Teachers do not suggest how it should happen. If this is the education show then it is as if the teachers are pulling participants out of the audience and showing them tricks that the selected audience members then perform. The show belongs to the audience. The Impresario hires teachers, or cast members, who accepted this kind of responsibility; responsibility for supporting the learning by the students, rather than the teaching by the teachers.

Teachers also run a leadership program that always has at least 150 students from the three grades. The leadership students do all of the organization for dances, all of the intramural activities, and all of the special events such as Halloween, Christmas, Welcome-Back Week, and others. Teachers stand beside the students and support them, but they do not run the events.

The students at Rosedale have sold the school to the community. Markum:

> This past weekend we had Run for the Cure. My receptionist and the students organized a district team of over 300 people, raised over $13,000.00. On the same day that we had a major sporting event in town and my students, along with students from George Thomson [the school across town] volunteered. Monday morning I got a call saying, "Do you want to know how wonderful these students are that you have?"

Markum accepts this kind of feedback from the community as proof that his approach is working. "Let's give them some authority. Let them do things." He shares authority and responsibility with staff and students, and in so doing he provides opportunities for them to learn how to deal effectively with both authority and responsibility.

Another major factor that has influenced the test results is the implementation of the International Baccalaureate (IB) program, an international program of the World School. It is a high demand program. Despite the ready availability of an Advanced Placement (AP) program at Rosedale and a neighbouring school, between 40 and 60 students were still being bused to a neighbouring city to attend the International Baccalaureate Program at two other schools. About eight years ago, one of the teachers at Rosedale investigated IB and suggested that Rosedale examine the possibility of offering the IB instead of the AP program. If Rosedale could attract those students back to their neighbourhood school, it would also increase funding to the school. The teacher volunteered to do the application and the staff put the information together. The administration of the school made a presentation to the board and asked permission to at least explore the possibilities. That much was granted; the exploration was completed and the application was made. It was successful and Rosedale implemented the program.

In the first year, 32 students entered the program. Markum describes these students as "just nice students." He did not see them as true IB material but the program had to start somewhere. In its seventh year the program has grown to 67 grade 10 IB students in three classes. In grade 11 there are two classes, and in grade 12 there is one full class of IB students. The program has definitely had an impact on the image of the school and on the academic results. It is like adding a high-wire act. It has improved the image and reputation of the school, its staff and the kind of student, or audience, it is able to attract.

Markum admits that previously the school, being a composite high school offering shop and work experience classes, was not considered a place for seriously academic students. With the IB program firmly in place and growing, there is no doubt that serious academics are welcome and students are encouraged to attend this local high school rather than choosing to go over the border into neighbouring districts. He explains, "What we were hoping we would do was pick up those students who wanted a real academic challenge from...surrounding areas and the numbers improved." The switch in programming has meant that the school's population is changing. The student population is becoming more academic, and as a result the school's average test scores are improving. There is a different kind of student writing the exams, so it only makes sense that the scores would improve overall. Other schools are on the same course, attracting new populations by implementing different programs such as IB to improve the image and increase the results. This, in turn, attracts a high quality student and creates a spiral of improvement for these schools.

Getting the Cast on the Right Page

The administrative team at Rosedale has been able to change the mind-set of the staff in the school. When Markum first arrived, it was at the request of the superintendent and the Board. He said no to them for years. He enjoyed his position at a junior high school across town. He had developed good relationships with the staff and community there and was rather comfortable, as he put it. He could not see the sense in moving from one junior high to another. But he was asked to come to Rosedale and he accepted. Paul's brother, who has been a high school teacher for more than 30 years, advised Paul to withdraw the application. His brother's description of high school teachers was less than complimentary. He called them "assholes." He warned Paul to stay away from them. Paul did not believe this assessment. Paul sensed that his brother had experienced such difficulty not only because he had made the switch to high school, but because he had moved from one part of the country to another and was forced to learn a new culture and adapt to a new community and a new school. Paul, on the other hand, was not leaving his community or moving to a different culture. He knew this community. His brother insisted that he knew the truth about high school teachers.

Not long into his first year at Rosedale, Paul came to understand the basis of his brother's words. Markum became convinced that it was due to the fact that these teachers in high school were teaching curriculum and not students. Some teachers cared about the students in the classes but few took the time to get to know them as people. If students did not perform at a certain level, they were asked to go to the office and get a drop sheet that would get them out of the class they were having trouble in and into something else. Markum insists that these teachers were nice people, but he feels that they did not understand that there was another way to approach students, learning, and academic success. With this in mind Markum and his team worked hard to promote the whole concept of teaching students not curriculum. After ten years he is proud to have staff members that are teaching students first, curriculum second. Now the "who" comes before the "what."

Markum remembers the April meeting his first year at Rosedale. He insisted that teachers leave the doors to their classrooms unlocked so the students could enter the room. One teacher asked "What do I do if the students arrive 20 minutes late?" "Well, then you'll be teaching them for 47 minutes rather than none," Markum replied. That response was not looked upon very favourably. There was a great deal of resentment. Markum wonders if most of his staff thought he was misguided and did not really understand high school. That was true at the time, he admits. He knew nothing. He did not know what a credit was. He had never worked in a high school before this. What he knew was how the students who were locked out were feeling. He spent a lot of time cruising and opening doors. He wanted the students to understand that they were important. If he has done anything in this school over the past ten years, if he has changed anything, he has introduced a principle of caring for students. To illustrate his points he tells a story.

> A teacher would come down and would say da da da da and I would say, "Whoa! Let's back up. Where did you start this morning? Did you get out of bed, get a nice warm breakfast? What do you think the kid had? Where do you think the kid slept? Do you think the kid stayed at home? Do you think he might have slept in the car because the old man would not let him in the house?" The teacher would say, "What the hell are you talking about?" I said, "What do you know about the students? Nothing. There's your question. Why do you not try to get to know who he is and then maybe you would understand more." And I think if I have done anything in this school, I have taught teachers to think about students.

We do not all come out of the same chute every morning.
We are not all as fortunate.

Markum believes that all teachers should be forced to teach in elementary school before they are allowed to teach anything else. He has voiced that opinion in Rosedale so often that many are tired of hearing it from him. He believes that the attitudes of the teachers at Rosedale are beginning to change. According to Markum, it is not so much policy that has changed as practices. He has negotiated with his staff an understanding that he, as principal, works for the students first and for his staff and the community second. He reports that he makes sure that teachers understand that he will stand behind them as long as they are putting the students' well being and academic success first, the same way he does. This show belongs to Markum and he is fiercely protecting his audience from anything less than a caring, concerned performance from staff. Markum's staff has come to understand that it is not *their* school; it belongs to the students and to the community. His stance is that teachers and administrators are simply employees. It has taken a long time to get this message across to some staff members from the old culture. He negotiated this perception through many hours of conversation and staff meetings. He had to be relentless and persistent in order for some of his staff to finally accept or at least comply with this underlying philosophical change.

Rewriting the Program

Like all principals in his province, Markum was asked to implement a change in the reporting structure to the Department of Education. A new accountability framework requires principals to report exam results in business plans to the department through the school division every year. Markum admits that Rosedale staff act on the results of these reports, and the actions are good for students. He sometimes becomes frustrated when he reads the Fraser Report, which takes the same data that he has collected from exam results and publishes them in the newspaper. Parents come in and ask what is going on. Markum believes that his staff show in their reports how they include all the students in the statistics.

He sees what he calls a disconnection between what the parents understand from the newspapers and what the teachers are able to show them in the school. Straightening things out takes energy.

Being a composite high school provides wonderful opportunities to do important things for all the students, not just the bright ones. All students' results are included in the reported statistics, which sometimes skews the reported averages. There is a Knowledge and Employability Program (K&E) at Rosedale, for example. The students in this program are usually lower functioning and struggle through school. At Rosedale between 30 and 50 percent of the K&E students finish with the certificate of achievement and a diploma. When students from K&E are writing diploma exams, the results are not expected to be as good as those of the average student. At Rosedale, the belief is that every student deserves to have a chance. When a student enters K&E, the staff works with them, quickly, to identify strengths and weaknesses. If the student is in a position to move up a level, he or she is given that opportunity. The timetable is constructed so that students changing streams can be accommodated. Scheduling requires that the staff consider all kinds of combinations and permutations. Markum gives an example of the flexibility that typifies the consideration of each student as an individual with different needs. "This year I have probably eight or nine grade 12s doing K&E this semester and English 20-2 next semester. They will come back the first semester of the following year and do English 33 and Social 33."

It has become important to emphasize the individuality of the school's programming in the Results Review prepared for the board. Administration of the district recognizes that there are differences in and amongst schools. It is difficult for Rosedale to compete academically with a school such as George Thomson, the academic school across town, when Rosedale offers more of the lower level courses in order to satisfy their population. The IB program certainly heightens the profile in the academic streams for Rosedale and balances the impact of the other programs. Rosedale has become very competitive as a result. Markum is proud that Rosedale is no longer the Tech School or the Voc Ed School.

21

It is Rosedale Composite High School with a "kick ass program" according to Markum.

One of the things that amazed Markum when he came to Rosedale was the detailed analysis of diploma results. For Markum, the accountability framework has meant that the analysis has been formalized and requires more thought and consideration of details. It does not permit generalization the way it had in the past. From that perspective he believes that policy changes concerning accountability have been a positive influence on education, teaching and learning. The documents help focus on what is of concern and give Markum the opportunity to take care of the concern. Markum believes that the accountability framework has benefits. He reports that the paperwork has proven to be a frustrating activity but the benefits are clear: it provides opportunities to effect change with data that back up the need for the proposed change. The Results Review, in particular, requires that he, as principal, report discrepancies in academic performance and any other anomalies in the statistics. By insisting that schools report and therefore pay attention to these things, the administration legitimizes a principal's concern around discrepancies that could possibly provide evidence of staff concerns, as well as student concerns.

New education planning or Results Review policies, mandated from the province, had some influence on how Markum has implemented his planned change. He does, however, do what is important for students, and the planning and the reviews provide an opportunity to examine more closely those things that need to be changed. The results reports provide him with the ammunition needed to implement changes with less resistance from an entrenched staff. Going back to the Impresaio metaphor, you might say that when ticket sales are low, it is easier to introduce changes to the act and to the program in an effort to promote the show to a wider audience and increase attendance. Adding a greater level of audience participation (students first) and a new high-wire act (the IB program) is readily accepted by the rest of the cast because they understand the importance of increased ticket sales (funding) to the continued success of the show.

Sharing the Dream

For a number of years, Markum was concerned about negative results on surveys from support staff about the opportunity for professional development—specifically for computer training—and about discipline. Apparently, support staff felt the discipline left a lot to be desired. Support staff includes clerical staff and teacher-aide staff. Markum confides that some teacher aides working in the K&E had long believed that if the principal did not take the students and "hang them from the second balcony" the discipline was not severe enough. This group of teacher aides proved to be the greatest challenge for Markum as he worked to win over the staff and change the culture of the school. The hard data provided by the survey results legitimized for Markum an opportunity to ask the aides about their discontent.

> *Okay you're not happy. What are we going to do about it? How do you think we can make things work for you? You want computer training, we have had two people here who volunteered their time and you have never signed up. So what is it about computer training that you need? You do not think that the discipline is up to snuff because we have not taken anybody in and had an execution. That is not going to happen. If you are having PMS, do not take it out on these students. So where do we go?"*

Things are getting better, according to Markum. His honest, open approach demands that everyone takes responsibility for his or her own fate. Some people react well to his approach. Markum and his staff provided the computer training that the disgruntled support staff wanted, and he also sent them out for specialized training as they had requested. Other support staff members are beginning to change their perceptions of him, and their own behaviour, through his continued negotiation with them.

Measuring Success

Markum identifies the move to a focus on the students as compelling evidence of the connection between leadership practices of principals and improving the results of students on standardized tests. The focus provides students with more opportunity and gives them more confidence. He admits that the fact that students in his school are spending more time in front of teachers now instead of in hallways might influence the test results. Other data on number of graduates per grade 12 class provides further evidence of the improvements. Markum's school has 250 graduating students. One of Markum's administrators, a dedicated man, scrutinizes the graduation lists and meets with most of the students who have problems with schedules or are in danger of not meeting the graduation requirements. He talks to them about their graduation needs, and he has a spreadsheet on every student. With the help of this administrator, Markum confidently reports that, "We have made a real conscious effort to find any way we can to make sure a kid at least gets a diploma, if nothing more."

Markum provides examples of what "any way we can" means to staff at Rosedale. It means that a student may have to repeat the Science 24 course because it is a diploma requirement. It means that students earn credits through the Registered Apprenticeship Program. The apprenticeship program allows students to earn credits in high school and at the same time receive credit for six months in an apprenticeship. The school is committed to getting students to complete their high school diploma. That does not mean that every student is eligible for post-secondary and certainly not all qualify for university entrance. Although the community expects that most will go to university, that is not realistic in Markum's mind. The bottom line is that all students who complete the requirements for the diploma get a base from which they can build a post secondary education or a career. He pushes, pulls and drags students across that graduation finish line.

The focus at Rosedale is beyond the standardized test scores. Markum sees a danger in focusing on just those diploma courses with standardized tests. He feels that the rest of the program would suffer if that were the case, and students would not be well served.

That is not to say that Rosedale does not focus on the diploma results. They do. It is clear that the whole picture includes, but is not limited to, the data provided in those standardized test results. Markum suggests that Rosedale takes pride in working for all the students, not just the academic ones. They have a Gaining Occupational Life Skills (GOLS) program that gives students opportunities to experience independent living. These students might live in group homes now, or may move to one following the program. Markum explains, "We try to get the students out of their family home because mom and dad are going to get older and then they're going to die. Then what the hell will these students do?"

Data on how many Rosedale students work in the community points to their success. Local businesses such as restaurants, hotels and bakeries have students working to earn credits and gain experience. Speaking about one student in particular who has been working as a dishwasher at a restaurant in town for 3 or 4 years, Markum comments, "She is diligent. They love her, she loves the work, and she loves the responsibility." The GOLS Program has been very successful for students such as the one Markum describes. The teacher who took over the program seven years ago has worked hard to get the students past high school and into local colleges. The goal is to have them start to live independently.

Increased teacher time, another factor contributing to the success, has not only happened as a result of students actually attending classes. The academic staff is available to the students before and after class as much as possible and to varying degrees. Some teachers are at the school before classes start, at noon and after school. The rest of the staff rarely see them because they are in their classroom working with students. Other students find it very hard to catch a teacher. Markum knows that students need to understand the teacher's involvement in other parts of the school and what they can offer. If the teacher is coaching football every night from 3:00 to 5:30, he or she is likely not going to be available at 2:30 to help a student. A student is held responsible for finding the teacher before school or at lunchtime. Consideration of a teacher's time is something Markum wants to instil in students. Although in junior high there are coaching duties, in a high school there are many more extra-curricular activities that staff support, so everyone on staff is very busy. There are still some teachers, Markum admits, who walk in at five minutes to 8:00 in the morning and walk out at 2:31 in the afternoon and consider that they had done a good day's work. "But I do not think you or I are going to change that." He chuckles.

Casting the Show

Markum admits that other department heads and principals believe that everybody should teach everything and that everybody has to take a turn teaching the lower level courses. Philosophically, Markum disagrees. He thinks that having teachers teach outside of their comfort zone is counter-productive. He refers back to his days of teaching junior high with a particular teacher who was a brilliant mathematician. That teacher could take 40 academic students at once and perform miracles. Markum, on the other hand, would take 15 or 18 of the weakest students and do mathematical magic with them. The mathematician could not do the same magic with the weaker students. He cared about them, and he could coach them on a sports team, but he was not able to relate to them in the math classroom.

Markum's belief is that teachers ought to be assigned where they are best suited or most compatible with the students to get the "...best bang for your buck." He says, "I have specifically gone out and got a couple of junior high guys [teachers] to do my K&E and my 14-level math/sciences because they are the ones who understand those kids." Markum is committed to finding the right match between the teacher and the program.

> *Why would I take my top science guy who has written the chemistry book that we use and put him in a 14 classroom? Because it is his turn? He is not going to give the students what they require. The students are going to hate him because he is too smart. So why do that?*

His teachers appear to enjoy the programs they teach, and they enjoy the students. The new recruits have expressed happiness with the transition to teaching in the high school environment. When

Markum arrived at Rosedale teachers were taking turns with the 14-level classes. He suggested that a different approach would mean happier staff and more successful students. "Let's find staff who best suit the program, and lets go from there." This is an interesting approach, counter to what others are doing; cross-training science teachers so that they can teach all levels, for example. Markum takes pride in finding the best person for the specific job, in contrast to focusing on training specialists in order to offer a broader range of courses.

Another example of matching staff and students for optimum performance is a program Rosedale offers called Transitional Recommended Year (TRY-10). The program is aimed at grade 9 students who are not quite ready for grade 10. The qualifier for the program is that they enrol in mainstream courses leading to regular classes. It is a low-enrolment program that has had as few as 20 students with two teachers. The teachers complement each other. Markum describes them as a teacher from junior high and a teacher who has taught high-level English in high school. "She can teach anybody," he adds proudly. According to Markum the two teachers work magic with the students in the program. At the end of the first year of the program the students made themselves T-shirts, with TRY "Totally Radical Year" on the front of them, which explains how the students feel about the experience. The program runs only in years when there are enough students. Some parents are reluctant to have their children enrol because they believe that the program is a special-needs program. The difference is in the level of courses offered. Consideration is given to adding Applied Math instead of the Math 14 to the program, which helps get rid of the stigma of dead-end courses. The program is for at-risk students and is meant to give them a leg up and get them back into the mainstream as soon as they are ready. Like the differentiated programming and mastery learning at other schools, this program offers second chances.

There are a variety of programs tailored to meet the needs of the students. This seems to lend credibility to Markum's claims of a shift in focus from teacher to student needs. At the same time his commitment to having the right teacher in the right place speaks to his concern for teachers as well. Markum identifies "Common sense and courtesy" as the only school rule. This rule has been applied in the development of programs and in the decisions on staffing; casting the right actor for the right role in his show.

Tacit Support from the Producers

Markum believes that his strong parent group and his highly qualified teaching staff work together very well to contribute to the success of students on standardized tests. Markum describes parent involvement as a critical factor contributing to the success of the school. Rosedale has a very positive relationship with the community and Markum admits to working hard to develop that over the years he has been at Rosedale. He recognizes that parents do not volunteer at high school very often, mostly because volunteers at Rosedale are asked to stuff envelopes, or make phone calls to inform parents of the interview times that have been set up with the teachers. The small number of volunteers in the school is not an indication of lack of support, according to Markum. In fact parents' absence is seen as support for a job well done. Markum takes pride in the fact that his community supports his school, citing their absence as evidence of their tacit commitment and support

Although the parent interviews are well attended, the work to convince parents that it is important to be a part of their child's education, even when that child has become a teenager, continues. Teachers run interviews or are available for drop-ins from 2-5 pm or 6-9 pm on the first day and 5-9 pm on the second day. Adding those hours to regular school hours adds up to about 10-hour-days for teachers. The art teachers, the communications technology teachers and other teachers who offer option courses usually do not have as many interviews, but the core subject teachers are busy for the entire time. Markum sees this as a great way to connect with parents or at least give them an opportunity to connect. Other schools invite students to attend the parent-teacher interviews, but at Rosedale this is not the case. Students are not necessarily invited to attend the interviews. Some do attend, but the school does not encourage it. Perhaps it is more important to provide the opportunity to talk about the progress students are making throughout the term than to mandate the students' attendance at interviews.

A closer look at the staff reveals informed, motivated and involved teachers; a staff that parents can put their confidence in and can support. One teacher wrote the text for chemistry and others have won teaching awards. Markum reports that the staff regularly reviews new curriculum. The staff from Rosedale is involved with ministry initiatives. One of the assistant principals is the coordinator of Special Needs in the school, and he accompanied Markum and one of their key teachers to talk to the committee reviewing special-needs programming. The staff volunteers to pilot new programs as they become available so that they can keep ahead of the curriculum changes. One of the social studies teachers has been seconded to the ministry. He has spent one year in assessment and one year in curriculum development and will be there for another two years. Markum expects that upon his return he will have considerable knowledge to share with his peers.

Rosedale has a number of staff members working on a variety of programs. The English department at Rosedale has been very involved in the development of the new English curriculum. The department head is one of the key people in the design and implementation. Her involvement is certainly encouraged. Markum acknowledges that he believes that it is better to be a part of the solution than to complain. He recognizes that the English program is an improvement over the previous program. It has been very well received by teachers. Markum expresses his commitment to this kind of on-going professional involvement, which he feels better prepares teachers for delivering the curriculum that is tested on the standardized tests. Parents and students can feel confident that they are being well served by a professional staff committed to ongoing professional development.

The Rosedale staff and community became particularly politically active with a newly introduced math program. The staff and the community did not believe that it was appropriate for teachers to receive the books in August and be asked to implement a new program without having had some in-service training or even some input into the final product. They demanded some answers.

The program proved to be flawed in the end. It was less the program and more the process of implementation that was questioned by the parents and staff at Rosedale. Either way, changes that occurred later justified this initial stance by the school community at Rosedale.

Teachers, school boards and universities were consulted after the program had been published for implementation, instead of before. Teachers were insulted. Markum believes that there is a misconception about teachers, that teachers are unwilling to accept change or that they are afraid of change. The truth, he believes, is that teachers will accept change if it is going to improve opportunities for students. The mistake, according to Markum, with the implementation of the new math program, was not including the stakeholders in the process of implementation.

Markum has always believed that it is really important to be on the cutting edge of change. As a teacher, he was one of the first to volunteer for a pilot. The pilot programs come with books to try and materials to test. Publishers are very generous when they think that their text might be chosen for the province. When they are part of the pilot, teachers are in a position to examine the materials and suggest an appropriate text. Markum remembers one new science program he piloted years ago at the junior high level; he had three very different teachers pilot three different texts for the new program. He insisted that they meet at the end of each unit of study to discuss the merits and drawback of each text. It was amazing. The cross-analysis of the text books meant that when it was time to make a decision they were ready, and their decision held for the district as a whole. Markum believes that teachers will never know the textbook unless they work through it. Merely looking at it, flipping through pages and seeing pretty pictures does not provide a teacher with a realistic perception for how it will work in the classroom. Markum believes strongly that it is very important to be in on the ground floor of those curriculum decisions. He negotiates perceptions of the control over curricular decisions and priority for pilot programs. He also makes expectations for teachers clear. At the same time, he negotiates perceptions of the impact of not using the pilot material, the significance of his approval and the risk of not complying with ongoing curricular development. Working with parents (his production crew), and his teachers (his performers), Markum, as promoter, strives to create the best show possible.

Renewing the Cast

Markum returns to the discussion of the IB program when he thinks about professional development. "One of the things that IB forces schools to do is train the teacher. I think what it has probably done for us is remind us how important professional development is to teachers." IB program regulations require that teachers receive training as part of the certification. However, the credentialing process and the specific training is expensive and usually far away. Markum smiles and says that teachers do not really feel burdened by being chosen to go to nice places and learn new things. The insistence from the program administrators forces the staff to consider their own professional development and to begin to question whether or not they ought to be sharpening the saw more often.

One limiting factor in the professional development of staff is the finances. The attitude toward funding professional activities for staff at Rosedale is that no one should be out of pocket if he or she is traveling for professional development. Therefore, sending more people is definitely more expensive than it might be in other schools where teachers contribute, at least in part, to their expenses. The budget is flexible and, although it may mean fewer texts or supplies, if it is important for a teacher to attend, then all of their expenses are covered.

An Impresario with Heart

Markum meets with all of his staff to discuss their teacher growth plans. With more than 80 teachers, devoting only one half hour to each represents one full week of his time. He admits that it is very time consuming but emphasizes that it is well worth the effort. Markum uses these one-on-one conversations to talk about life in the classrooms and any goals the teachers may have set for themselves. He also uses the time to connect with them at a more personal level. "If I got somebody who's got cancer then we talk about that. Because that is what is important." He believes that teachers who might be overwhelmed with personal issues cannot give their full attention to their job. He sometimes accepts the role of counsellor in order to get teachers to a place where they can be effective in the classroom.

It is evident that Markum loves what he does. He is what others might describe as a people person. He is eligible for retirement, but he is not prepared to suggest when he might retire. He says he thinks it would not be anytime soon.

> *...I am 55 ye ars old. What the hell am I going to do? I do not like reading. I do not have a woodworking shop at home that I can go and while-away the time. I do not have hobbies except fishing. I do not have anybody to go fishing with. My father-in-law died a couple of years ago so what the hell am I going to do?*

Markum always says that when the students do not want him around anymore he will go home. He reports that at the last graduation, almost half of the students stopped to hug him as they received their certificates. He has won over a number of teachers with his gruff, loving manner. His concern for students, teachers, parents and education is evident. He smiles. Markum reports shifts in staff's attitude and approach from a teacher-focus to a student-first focus. He has moved them from teachers of curriculum to teachers of students. He reports providing clear expectations for care and concern for students as individuals and for teachers as individuals. He makes responsibilities clear. He also makes clear the circumstances of accountability for staff. His perception is, "If the teachers are happy they work harder. They work harder, the students are happier. The students work harder, the parents are happier. It really works well. But it is the little things that make the big things count." Markum seems to be one of those big things that have made the little things count.

The show is over. Another performance concluded. The stands are empty now, decorated with the litter and detritus of an audience that was captured and enthralled with the big show. Their participation echoes still in the walls of the arena, reminding the Impresario of why he engages in the production, as well as his love in taking the performers, and the audience, to heights they have never experienced before.

He takes a deep breath, and moving slowly off-stage he begins to imagine a new season, a new show and....

Characteristics of the Impresario:
- Charismatic
- Visible
- Honest
- Transparent
- Sharing
- Commanding
- Fun
- Respected

To be Effective the Impresario leader needs to:
- Acknowledge others
- Keep an open forum for expression
- Create opportunities in new and exciting environments
- Seek efficiencies
- Ensure people are in roles where they can thrive

To work with the Impresario others need to:
- Be prepared to take the good with the bad
- Be open to "going for the ride" on many potential opportunities
- Be prepared to work independently and to a high standard
- Put students first

Chapter 3: The Sherpa

Hepburn School

Slowly out of the mist at 22,000 feet the shadows emerge; the small hardy men who act as guides, protectors and porters for the high altitude Himalayan mountain expeditions. Their nut brown faces betray their Tibetan ancestry as well as their confidence. Sure footedness borne of decades of experience and expertise guides climbers up the most treacherous routes to the summits of such mountains as Everest or K2. Although they carry immense loads up incredibly challenging slopes Sherpas are most proud of their ability to act as guides, protecting their clients against the predations of the hostile environment while allowing those clients to conserve energy for the push to the summit. As expert guides, Sherpas command more respect and higher pay than others who act as mere porters.

The Mountain Climb

Ted Norquay, the Sherpa porter, is willing to do a lot of the heavy lifting at his school to ensure that teachers are not burdened by issues and duties that interfere with getting students to the individual summits of their secondary education. Norquay sees his efforts at "taking care of the little things" as the most important contribution he makes. He wants to take away from teachers any annoyances that might take their concentration away from the classroom. Norquay, as Sherpa guide, seems to be arranging for a climb where nothing can get in the way of success. Principal Ted Norquay is a man dedicated to service. He is a Sherpa on the mountain of education. He works quietly in the background, preparing teachers and students for a climb that can be successful only with his help and protection—protection from the predations of provincial politics and school division bureaucracy. For his efforts he receives little recognition.

Sherpa, Guide and Leader

At Hepburn School, Ted Norquay is the kind of principal who likes to have structure and harmony. An ex-music teacher with a PhD in religious studies, he is not your typical high school administrator. He is a quiet man who was promoted from the staff to the position of principal and he understands completely the frustrations of his teaching staff when faced with tasks and duties that distract from their chosen vocation of teaching. Perhaps because of this background and perspective Ted sees himself at the bottom of an inverted triangle, serving those who he leads by guiding and structuring their efforts to succeed with their charges—the students of Hepburn School.

This dedication to removing obstacles starts with the physical facilities. "What I try to do is make sure that the shop (the physical plant) is looked after. That is something that I can do. I feel I have the ability to do that—manage the technical part of running the school." As a recent classroom teacher he understands the importance of concentration and how very annoying it is to have desks in bad repair or technology that does not work; so, he does what he can to support the teachers by reducing the number of physical distractions. He reports doing little things such as coming in on a weekend to hook up a computer, fix a desk, or make sure the staff room is clean.

On the administrative side, Norquay explains that he spends time after school on paperwork, and he admits he is not sure that teachers know how much time he does spend. "If they were asked what I am doing to help them, I am not sure they would think of that because it has really become accepted. It would be like asking fish if they were in water or not," he laments. In his own mind he does not feel the staff acknowledge that things are different since he accepted the position of Principal. Norquay wonders how much they even appreciate the changes that he has been working on behind the scenes. "Anything that's aggravating and annoying them

I will try to remove that aggravation if at all possible." His selflessness, although apparently unacknowledged, is commendable.

This selflessness extends to taking over extra-curricular tasks that are normally carried out by teachers. As at other schools, teachers at Hepburn report a severe aversion to noon-hour supervision because it is

> "Anything that's aggravating and annoying them, [the teachers] I will try to remove that aggravation if at all possible."
>
> Ted Norquay, Sherpa

a half hour where they can meet or enjoy quiet time. Hepburn school used to have eight teachers supervising the cafeteria at noon hours. Now Norquay does the supervision of the cafeteria himself along with two teacher aides. In Ted's estimation, the cafeteria really does not have to be supervised. It just has to be kept clean. He has taken on the supervision because he sees it as one of those aggravations that he can easily remove. Norquay also sees this compromise around noon-hour supervision as a win/win situation. He likes to know what is going on in the building. He believes that the only way to know is to be moving through the school. The students are all in the cafeteria at lunch time, so being there affords him the opportunity and the advantage of finding out what is going on in the school from the students. There are still teachers on supervision in other parts of the school, but not nearly as many as there were before Ted came. By increasing the teacher aide time and taking on the lion's share of the supervision, he has removed one of the annoyances and aggravations he feels gets in the way of teachers' satisfaction with the job. Norquay believes this is a good example of a leadership style that he identifies as collaborative. He appears to be very willing to do more than his share and to make sacrifices or accommodate others for the sake of peace and harmony in the school. However, it does come at a cost: because his time is taken up by the extra tasks, he is not available for the informal encounters with teachers in the staff room.

On the Mountain of Education

Ted Norquay, now managing a relatively large organization called a school, recognizes that a critical part of facilitating teachers and students in achieving their goals is ensuring that the school organization has the structure, systems and processes in place for information to flow well in support of the coordination of activities. He has been principal for four years. Much of that time has been spent clarifying expectations of students, of teachers, of support staff. Clarifying the rules and administrative processes has also been important. Ted has invested much time in creating efficient processes to facilitate the repetitive basic administrative procedures required to support teachers in their jobs. Processes such as the application to go on leave, go on a field trip, or to request a vehicle are structured to clarify expectations and ensure smooth operations. The time he spends on these basic foundational policies and structural arrangements is meant, once again, to ease the burden on teachers by removing unnecessary administrative complexity and complications that might drain their energy. Ted explains, "This is something that I can do. I know how to do it and I make sure it is happening."

As a Principal, Norquay emphasizes his desire and a commitment to manage by walking around:

> *I try to be out and about, I guess that is a part of it, actually. The thing that is important as a leader, as a principal of a school, you cannot get stuck in this room. You have got to somehow be wandering around the school as much as possible. So I will do my work at home. My computer is hooked up at home and I do all my emailing at home. I do all my grading at home or I come in early in the morning and weekends. So that is quite demanding but when I am here at school I am rarely in my office.*

As a leader Ted is very clear about his values and own agenda. "There are things that I believe in and I do push them," he explains. This does not mean he falls on the autocratic side of the leadership decision-making scale. He is very aware that his ideas about the future of education and Hepburn School have to be supported by a critical mass of staff in order to become a reality. "I always do check that I have a few allies or I know it is not going to work." He also is proactive in seeking and soliciting ideas from his staff, especially when those ideas are synergistic with his vision for the school's future. Ted continually watches for suggestions from a teacher or teacher aide that he believes would benefit the school, and then he does everything he possibly can to help make sure the idea receives the support needed to reach implementation.

When it comes to the relationships between himself and his staff in general, Ted holds to two very strong principles. He feels that his relationships with all staff has to be founded on respect and civility, no matter how much he might differ with some staff in personality and in ideas. Secondly, Ted feels he is obligated to seek and recognize a kernel of truth in any idea that is presented to him, even if he is in disagreement with the idea or the manner in which the idea is presented. The values of mutual respect, civility and transparency are important to him as a leader, and he believes these values underpin the evolution of a distinctive culture for Hepburn School.

The Routes: Guiding Change

Perhaps the greatest test for a leader of any organization is leading change. Norquay's story of how and why he has been able to make some changes in what he describes as a well-entrenched math department is compelling. He read a study that identified four attributes of teachers whose students score well on Math Provincial Achievement Tests (PATs). The findings from the study indicated that the teachers in the study were 1) all math majors; 2) they had all taught for at least five years; 3) they were are all engaged in professional activities such as marking exams; and 4) they knew the curriculum from top to bottom. The fourth finding, knowing the curriculum from top to bottom, is of particular interest to Norquay.

In the school, there had been what he describes as a hierarchy. Teachers who were math majors were assigned math courses. They did not necessarily have experience teaching math. Once they were teaching math they would "work their way up" to Math 30, which was a career "summit" for math teachers, "By the time you taught here for 20 years you might be given the privilege of teaching math 30" explains Norquay. He further explains that the goal of the exercise for math teachers was to teach only Math 30 and nothing else. Once teachers were doing that, they had status.

Norquay became convinced that having only one person teach a particular subject and level is not good for that person or for the students. He learned through a study that teachers who are familiar with different levels of math, and have taught them, are more successful math teachers. After finding this study, Ted began to introduce the concepts to his math department. Four years later he was still working towards having each teacher teach all the grade levels from 9 to 12. His agenda became to change the old mind set and move teachers towards a broader base of curriculum knowledge. His goal was to have a 9 through 12 math team. Although he was aware of the need, resistance to a sea change in culture in the math department remained strong. An opportunity to introduce change appeared from an unlikely direction—declining enrolments.

Declining enrolments have previously been interpreted as unfortunate. The opportunity that Norquay found in the declining enrolments was that he could legitimately say to the math teachers, "Look, either you are going to have to teach math across grade levels, or, if you insist on just teaching grade 12 you are going to have to teach science because there is not enough math left just to teach grade 12 math." That was how he approached it. He felt strongly that by creating math teams he could address the test results in math. The study he read indicated that teachers cannot really teach grade 9 math well unless they teach math 30. The rationale is that it is important to understand where the students are headed in their study of math.

For Norquay, the change in the math department is a prime example of where a leader can develop a clear direction in response to the facts (the study) then take advantage of an opportunity (declining enrolment) to achieve the appropriate change to gain better results for the school. Ted believes that "the trick in leadership is to see the opportunity." If there had been increasing enrolments, the same opportunity would not have existed. Norquay feels that

being able to identify and exploit the opportunity is an aspect of leadership where he excels.

Ted is proud that the change he has led in the math department has had a specific impact on the culture of the grade 9 class as well. It had been generally accepted, for reasons unexplained, that the grade 9s needed tight control. At some point in the history of the school, a decision was made to deal with this problem by assigning one teacher to each of the core subjects at the grade 9 level. Each of the four teachers specialized in and taught one subject. The result was that every grade 9 student had to take a course from each of these four teachers.

Norquay describes these teachers as having very similar approaches to managing their classrooms, an approach that can best be described as highly authoritarian and controlling. As a result of this disciplinarian culture many grade 9 students were afraid of their teachers. When it came to writing provincial exams these students did not care how well they did. When they were asked about it they would say, "Why do we want to make this teacher look good?" Doing poorly on the exams meant little to them except where it gave them a chance to get even for what they had interpreted as unfair treatment at the hands of their teachers. Norquay believes that this attitude of revenge on the part of the students played a major role historically in the results on the grade 9 exams. More importantly, the grade 9 students, although well supervised and disciplined, might not have been getting the academic background they would later need to do well at other grade levels. Teachers who teach at many different grade levels came to the grade 9 classes without any assumptions about behaviour. Students began to respond in different ways as they were exposed to different teaching styles and approaches, and they became more engaged. From Norquay's perspective these students became interested in making their teachers look good, and so they worked hard to do well on the exams.

As a Sherpa guide, Norquay observes that having student climbers who want to climb the mountain is key for success. You cannot drag people to the summit, no matter how good you think the experience will be for them. Critical for the motivation to move towards the summit is the relationship established between student and teacher. As Sherpa leader Norquay realizes he can make the organizational arrangements that will increase the odds of the best teacher/student relationship occurring. This, in turn, increases the students' chance of success.

A Mountain of Paperwork

Since his elevation to the leadership of the school Ted has waged a tough, continuing battle, not with staff or students, but with central office administration for the school division. Ted's intent, carried out with a quiet anger, is to protect his staff from the dizzying array of reports and bureaucratic routines imposed on his school by the District. Among the documents required by the district are reports on local school progress; these reports are added to a district system report. The system report itself identifies issues such as partnerships, health authority relationships, building plans, special growth plans, etc., that have to be written up. Separate from the system reports are required reports documenting provincial exam results and improvement plans, as well as strategy management plans. The plans, the reports, the gathering of data and the consequent analysis, the forms, the templates—all these add up to a bureaucratic burden that Ted describes as "a little overwhelming". Just reading the documentation from the district is a challenge, let alone responding to it.

Imbedded in many of the reports are performance measures that are expected to be updated regularly throughout the year. The measures and formats for reporting are standardized so that comparison between schools throughout the district, and indeed the whole system, is possible. Norquay makes every effort throughout the school year to keep track of measures he knows will be expected in the reports. Ted takes these measures seriously as he has linked them directly to priorities in improving learning in Hepburn School. "At every staff meeting, I give the staff our priorities and ask them to mention what we have done this month to advance those priorities," he says. In this way a provincial mandate handed down through the district becomes linked to test score improvements.

Feedback from parents is also part of the reporting system, but in this School District, the annual survey is a challenge. Surveys of grade 9 and 12 parents are administered at the end of every year. Ted is expected to hire teacher aides out of his school budget because 250 families have to be contacted by phone. Once the teacher aides have contacted the families and gathered the information, he and other staff members develop a results report which takes a considerable amount of time. To improve the process to implement the survey, Norquay has set up a system to collect data for the survey results report throughout the year. He identifies this as a key accomplishment, part of what he described earlier as "keeping the store clean" or "maintaining a tight ship". "I learned after a year or two, I had better be doing this throughout the year. There is no way I could pull this together at the end. So if I developed these routines to do that and not bother the teachers with this..." Once again Ted demonstrates his intent to allow the teachers to focus on their work with students rather than be distracted by imperatives that are imposed from the District.

A major source of frustration for Ted is a continual cycle of requests from the District, often on short notice, for improvement plans. These requests, plus a tendency for the District Superintendent to pressure Ted for results, have become a source of friction between Norquay and the District Office. "We have improved, but we have never pulled it together that way so that I could just put into the three pages what they require. I do not have those in a drawer some place where I can just pull them out and give them to central office." Norquay, nonetheless, spends a considerable amount of time preparing reports for special events like District Board meetings. Rather than bother his teachers he has taken on the job of justifying improvements himself. He is not happy about it and he says so, but he does what he can to get the information together and to the superintendent in a timely fashion. "I take it upon myself to say 'Look, you guys, if you want improvement plans, fine, but tell me sometime earlier than two days ago that you are going to want these.' To me this is where I think I would have a legitimate criticism of the leadership above me".

The reporting of exam results is one example of what Ted finds frustrating about the paperwork that faces him throughout the seemingly endless cycle of documentation. The results reflect a deep difference in philosophy and outlook, which puts him at odds with the District and perhaps the province. He is expected to put exam results in the Results Report and then he is also expected to put them in the Education Plan. He never understood the rationale behind reporting that information twice until he discovered that recording the exam results in two places means having exam results and participation rates in the same place.

Once he saw the two statistics together he became aware of why Hepburn's scores in Physics 30 have been consistently lower than the provincial average. He points out that high participation in Physics classes typically brings the average academic scores in Physics down. "I knew that we had these negative scores in physics but I want the participation rates to stay high. Generally speaking we have about twice as many students taking physics than in other schools." He mentioned this to the superintendent. It is this difference in philosophy that has created a negative impact on Hepburn's results.

> "Now to me this is not an excuse when I say to Mike (the superintendent), we are never going to get the same average as the province. Schools across the province teach physics to only one-quarter of the population. We teach physics to almost one-half of our population. "Our philosophy is I would rather have a kid in physics doing marginal work in grade 12 than sitting in the cafeteria or working for McDonalds."

Norquay especially does not understand why he should be expected to go to the teacher and ask for an improvement plan for these marks in Physics 30, with the participation rate being what it is. He feels strongly that students should have full schedules so that they are always learning something, even if they are not performing at the provincial average. "And that's what I said to Mike. We do not have an improvement plan and I do not intend to go get one." Norquay's assumption and personal philosophy is that teachers are always trying to improve. He believes that every teacher can be a good teacher. "So when you talk about accountability plans and whether they are of any value, in a way they are because it seems to me a good leader or a good teacher is always taking account of how we are doing and tries to do better and maybe that is our weakness. But we do not need this."

For Norquay, a key priority is to protect teachers from becoming overloaded, and he is not afraid to inform the district superintendent of his perspective. Ted acts as a protector and intermediary between "his" teachers and the machinations of the School District. He takes on the responsibility of informing the staff about what is happening in the District and at the provincial level so they are able to focus on what he views as the important priorities for students. For all the planning and reporting, Norquay sees teachers as working to improve learning directly with the students. "They just kind of go with something that is working with the students." As the school leader, Norquay sees his major role as supporting his teachers' success. He begins by measuring those successes. However, he recognizes that the *measure* of success, as determined at the local level in Hepburn, is at variance with the priorities and measures developed at the provincial and district level. "For example the completion rate; that is one of our priorities, and to me that is really important."

The dichotomy boils down to a provincial and district mandate to boost academic achievement scores, and Hepburn's aim to increase participation in academic classes—an initiative that seems to work against increasing academic scores by bringing average test scores down. The result is a mountain of paperwork that Norquay climbs alone, breaking a trail that teachers and students can follow without the added burden of cutting through the underbrush.

Reaching the Summit

Norquay has done his homework when it comes to defending his philosophy on completion rates. He looked at the age group of the students who should be graduating together in grade 12. He determined the range of their birthdays, assumed they would have entered grade 1 together and that most of those students would have graduated from Grade 12 at Hepburn. Taking into account students who have been kept back or moved, Norquay identified 114 students who ought to have graduated together. "There were 114 students and 53 percent of those 114 students ended up crossing the stage at graduation." He was surprised by this low graduation rate.

Armed with this information Norquay began to investigate why the other 47 percent did not graduate. What he found was, "about 20 percent of them dropped out. I think they are still in town. They are still hanging around. They did not move away." There were roughly another 20 percent who did not qualify for a high school diploma. "They just have not kept up, they got behind someplace in grade 10 and grade 11 or whatever, just did not have homework assignments completed and just did not graduate with their peers." Earning the required 100 credits in the right courses that qualify students for graduation can be delayed by a failure in a course in any given year of school. Having to repeat the course can put students in a position where they may not be able to fix their schedules in a way that permits them to complete the requirements. Norquay is confident that these students will eventually graduate.

The last reason that students do not graduate from Hepburn surprised Norquay. He identified 11 students who refused to prepare an exit portfolio. "The exit portfolio is a requirement for graduation. These students have their high school diploma but they refuse to finish off the portfolio for many kinds of reasons. As a result they are not eligible to cross the stage with their peers." In the end, 60 students out of 114 graduated on time, meeting the requirements of the province for their diploma and the requirements of the district for the portfolio. To Ted, it seems that the district has put another completely unnecessary bureaucratic hazard on the mountain just before the summit.

Leadership in Thin Air

One area where Ted feels there is a huge gap is in gaining feedback from his teaching staff on his performance as a leader. Because of union regulations, this kind of feedback is difficult to survey. This is true not only for Ted but for every principal who is a member of the teachers' professional association. The principals often find themselves operating in a vacuum as far as their leadership performance is concerned. "I would be very interested to hear whether or not they see what I am doing. I really wonder about that..." Ted recognizes that he has shouldered a lot of responsibility behind the scenes in order to take administrative burdens from his staff and to protect them from bureaucratic pressures, but he has no real feel for whether his efforts are appreciated or supported.

Ted has received some informal criticism from his staff. There is a sense that they feel their concerns and issues are not being heard. Their perception is that school issues do not get resolved, that issues are "left lying around". Norquay disagrees with this criticism. He feels that he does listen. There are situations, however, where he feels he cannot reveal the actions he is taking behind the scenes. He is also aware that progress on certain issues is slower than many teachers expect. Norquay has a large staff and he feels that meeting all of their competing demands is beyond anyone's reach. Yet he remains committed to trying. "There is never a straight line so you really have to pay close attention. That is the best I can offer." From Ted's point of view, these staff members expect that a motion at a meeting and a vote is a way of addressing issues. They think that once a vote is taken, the issue will be dealt with and they can move on.

Norquay identifies this democratic voting approach as very corporate and bureaucratic. He does not buy in to that type of procedure. "We have no votes here," he announces proudly. He believes in decision making by building consensus. The leader sets direction and gains input from staff, then they make decisions together and act accordingly. The major challenge Norquay faces is that consensus building and action take time—time for communicating, building relationships with stakeholders, and constructing the consensus on which to take action. Ted has very little time for such political action because he is completely occupied carrying the administrative burdens as well as "protecting" his staff from the pressures generated from the District. His staff members are indeed left unburdened, and they are "protected", but essentially they are on their own in working with the students at Hepburn

School. The staff have little idea of the work Ted is doing in the background, and thus little appreciation for his efforts on their behalf. Ted is simply a Sherpa porter carrying the administrative burden while the teachers get students up the mountain of education.

The irony of the situation is that despite Ted's philosophical differences with the district, and the provincial focus on test scores, the test scores at Hepburn school are improving. Perhaps because Ted's efforts left them free to focus on their students, the teachers at Hepburn school are able to assist their charges in gaining higher academic achievement scores. In the end, however, the personal cost to Ted is beginning to show. He is not a happy man, and the stresses of the work and unrecognized personal sacrifice are beginning to show in his demeanour and physical presence. We see Ted in a snippet of time and cannot help but wonder how long he can carry on as a Sherpa-style leader labouring up the mountain of education.

The Sherpas pass by, their bodies bent under the tremendous loads they carry in the high, thin air over the steep, icy and treacherous slopes of the mountain. As they appeared, they disappear, inevitably swallowed in time by the mists swirling at the higher elevations.

Characteristics of the Sherpa:
- Dedicated
- Harmonious
- Efficient
- Selfless
- Detailed
- Individualist
- Sacrificing
- Invisible

To be Effective the Sherpa needs to:
- Manage time well
- Be organized and structured
- Prioritize carefully
- Seek ways to streamline work processes and paperwork
- Delegate tasks as appropriate

To work with the Sherpa others need to:
- Take responsibility for completing their work
- Acknowledge the "heavy lifting" of others
- Manage expectations
- Support where possible

Chapter 4: The Coach

Adelaide High School

"Bottom Line of Coaching: *Interacting with another person so that an ability shows up 'over there' in their action.*"
- James C. Selman, *Coaching Beyond Management*

Exuding a quiet confidence the Coach paces the sidelines. He does not say much except for the occasional shout of encouragement or a small correction. He trusts and respects the players in the team, knowing that they can "read" the situation on the field and adjust as the changing circumstances dictate. He knows he cannot direct the players on the team, like chess pieces on a field, but must allow them to do their best within a carefully cultivated culture of accountability. All players on the team are supremely competent in their roles, and some of them have proven their status as "star".

However the team's quality ensures their continuing success on the field despite the changing dynamics of the game. This quality also allows them to respond to their ruthlessly results-oriented coach. Each player knows he or she is accountable for the team's results, which are calculated in myriad ways that monitor progress to the big score—the final score that is recognized as team success. Success attracts success, and the sustained top results of this team attract highly competent and star players from around the league. The Coach is responsible and accountable to the fans and the owners of the club for this sustained success. His fierce dedication to the players and to measurable results has made him a "star" in his own right.

The Playing Field

Adelaide Community High School is located in a small, remote community: a resort town with a transient population and a high level of interest in ecological and environmental concerns. Transportation costs make living here expensive, and the beautiful scenery makes it highly desirable. Adelaide is one of only 66 schools that received a charter giving it status as a "Community" School. Community Schools are given extra funding and responsibility. The responsibility is to bring the community to the school, with a goal of increasing the use of the school from 20 percent to 80 percent. The goal is for 80 percent of the town's population to use the school over the course of a year, and for the school building to be in use 80 percent of the time.

Though funding for community schools has dried up, the focus on the community is obvious at Adelaide. Nothing in the school happens without consideration of how the community can be involved. Nothing happens in the community without a consideration of how the school might be involved. The community owns the school and its programs. The school is protected by and serves the community, not just the parents. The entire community has a stake in the success of the school. As a result, the school is very responsive to the needs of the community.

Coach of Coaches

Rich O'Sullivan, principal of Adelaide High School, is a handsome man in his early fifties. He tends to dress casually, obviously more comfortable in sports wear then in the suit and tie that might go along with being a high school principal. He is athletic and seems at home in this resort town that offers so many ways to stay active. Although he seems totally relaxed and at home, even in the chaos that schools can reflect, his physical strength and presence command respect. Principal Rich O'Sullivan coaches his team of teachers toward educational success, success for him meaning measurable educational attainment by students. Top educational results represent a championship for O'Sullivan and this school. He uses his skills as a coach to instruct and encourage members of his teaching team. It is a unique team in a unique setting.

Focus on the Scores: Winning

Rich O'Sullivan places a critical importance on academic scores, so his team of teachers is clearly aware of the expectation that Adelaide students will do well on exam results. By focusing attention on these results, he influences teachers' understanding of the significance of test scores, especially the results on diploma exams. O'Sullivan believes that academic results are increasingly important to students, given the way post-secondary institutions are changing their requirements for enrolment and the resulting competition for entrance into

> *Working to improve academic results is the number one thing I can do as an administrator.*
>
> Rich O'Sullivan, Coach

the best schools. Although many teachers, perhaps even most teachers, would rather not have the diploma exams, O'Sullivan accepts that they are a fact of life: "The test scores are one way of measuring how our students are doing, and providing we are doing a balanced assessment, they will tell us something. Working to improve academic results is the number one thing I can do as an administrator." O'Sullivan believes that a balanced assessment is the key to the future for his students, his teachers and the school. In using the term "balanced assessment" O'Sullivan includes school-awarded marks, which result from school test scores as well as other measures that reflect student knowledge and achievement. These school-awarded marks contribute 50 percent to the final graduating grade.

O'Sullivan strongly believes it is important to recognize that diploma exams test certain skills. Teachers are testing these same skills in the classroom using other assessment tools. Students need these different kinds of assessment or feedback, but ultimately they need to be prepared to write the kind of exam they face in the diploma examination room.

O'Sullivan also believes that after each administration of standardized tests, it is important for teachers to complete an evaluation or analysis of results. These evaluations include looking for anomalies and identifying areas of strength as well as areas that need to be improved. His clear expectations for evaluation and results analysis serve to focus staff on measurable outcomes but also, just as importantly, the methods of teaching they use that lead to those outcomes.

Anomalies of a Small Field of Play

At Adelaide School the number of students writing the exams at any given time is small but highly variable. This makes analysis tricky. The number of students writing a particular exam rarely exceeds 30 and might be as small as 8. The numbers can vary widely from semester to semester, but overall the small numbers mean that a low result from one or two students has an inordinately large impact on the school's overall grade average. Also, when numbers are small, the publication of results means that the students and the teachers come under considerable public scrutiny when test scores are published.

On the positive side, the advantage of small enrolments means that Adelaide teachers know the students very well. Because of their familiarity with each student, teachers often know, before the exams are written, how the students will do under the pressure of the diploma exam. It is relatively easy for teachers to explain, for any individual student, why things might have gone amiss on an exam or why a school-awarded mark might be significantly higher than a diploma mark or vice versa. The reasons for differences in exam performance can vary as much as individual students vary from each other. Reduced or low exam results might reflect a need for upgrading or an aversion to multiple choice tests, or a personal or family situation that is causing undue stress on a student's life. On the other hand, because of the small size of Adelaide's student population, it is harder to make raw judgments about how the students in the school are doing as a whole unless the results are examined over time. For this reason the staff at Adelaide analyze the five-year reports provided by the department as well as the results for each examination.

Placing emphasis on the exam results and examining the reasons behind any anomalies has helped this small school improve its average test scores. Once there has been some analysis, O'Sullivan follows up with the teachers to check on what they might be doing differently and whether or not they notice any change or improvement. This method of holding teachers to account is a more private and individual approach than the publication of the results, which serves as a public holding to account of teachers and students for results. Some of the teachers are very defensive about the publication of numbers because it reflects directly on them. If there is only one English teacher, one person responsible for teaching all 30-level students in that subject, and test scores are comparatively low, it is easy to point fingers in the direction of the one teacher. However, causes of lower averages are not always easy to trace to a single source, and teachers are right to point out that results depend to some degree on the ability and attitudes of students, which can change dramatically from year to year.

The administrative staff examine discrepancies between school-based marks and the provincial averages, and if they are low, the teacher and the administration participate in a conversation about why that might be happening. This type of conversation can be interpreted by some teachers as punishment, or at least consequences, for the less-than-expected results. Whatever the interpretation of the conversation, it is clear that teachers are being held to account for these discrepancies in results by the administration of the school.

Variations in how "tough" teachers are in their marking is another issue that is debated in Adelaide's results-oriented culture. Teachers who place a high value on proven achievement sometimes put themselves at a disadvantage when compared to teachers who might not be as insistent on academic rigour. Constantly raising the question of how students are evaluated serves to focus teachers on their evaluation strategies because they have come to understand that they can expect to be held to account, not only for mere results, but for the quality of education. In making this expectation clear, and through the continual debate, O'Sullivan seems to have heightened the teachers' interest in learning more about assessment and evaluation, more about the specific skills that can lead to better outcomes for students without sacrificing real achievement.

Skills Training

Each year, O'Sullivan encourages his teachers to participate in the marking process for provincial exams. O'Sullivan believes that the opportunity to work with colleagues who teach the same subjects, and to be a part of the marking process at the provincial level, is invaluable when it came to developing an understanding of how the students can be successful in achieving test results. This is especially true for teachers in small schools because they do not have colleagues they can share their experience with. The exposure to the tests and the other teachers is extremely important when there is only one teacher of a subject in a school.

Adelaide has teachers in English, Biology and Social Studies who have participated in the provincial exam marking. O'Sullivan believes that this is another way to make sure that the school is on the right track with its school-awarded marks. As a result of participating in the marking program, the teachers are sometimes asked to participate in field testing of new questions for the exams. This contributes to a greater understanding of the tests, their structure and their purpose for the teachers involved. O'Sullivan reports that the emphasis on exams and marking has encouraged teachers to adapt teaching behaviour in order to improve scores.

As a leader, O'Sullivan talks about the tests and the results frequently. He reports that he recently attended a workshop on interpreting diploma exam results. With his actions, he suggests that he is demonstrating the value that he places on exam results. At the workshop he became aware of some ideas that might improve the information that teachers have taken from the data to date. "They showed us a little trick about colour coding, and I think I will show that to people. I am not going to make them do it, but I think some will look at it and say 'this is for me'." Sharing the information from the workshop provides another opportunity to talk about exams with his staff.

O'Sullivan values the opportunity for conversations that permit him to negotiate the significance of the results with his staff. He sees results as a priority and wants the staff to view these results in the same way.

O'Sullivan gives credit to his teachers and describes them as conscientious. "They are always bugging me: 'When are the exam results coming?' 'Have you got the results?' When the results come in, they want to look at them right away. It seems to matter to them." His appreciation of their attitude is apparent.

Ranking: Scoring

As O'Sullivan describes the Results Reviews and education plans required by the province he likens having to produce the reports to a double-edged sword. "You can argue with or take issue with the ranking of schools. How do you know if you are comparing apples with apples all the time?" He is philosophical about the advantages and disadvantages of the system. The positive outcome for him is that more public accountability had led schools to study and learn from results. "People argue about whether it has increased or improved student learning or improved student results. Is there a difference between them? Who knows?" Whether or not student learning has improved in his school, it appears that the emphasis he places on test results has an impact on the test scores in his school. Scores are increasing, which is having an impact on the school's ranking.

O'Sullivan believes that administrators are getting better at crunching numbers because of the changes in funding structure at the ministry. They are better at interpreting data because of the need to understand the results. They need to understand results so that they can defend what is happening in their schools. O'Sullivan writes the Adelaide result reviews and education plans himself. His jurisdiction is not as prescriptive as others regarding what ought to be included. He predicts that the standards for plans and reviews might become tighter in the future. Questions are asked about the results, and explanations are expected. The future seems to hold more documented accountability for Adelaide. This increased demand is okay with O'Sullivan.

Whether or not this demand for more detail is the accountability called for by the change in provincial policy, this is how the policy impacts principals in their schools. Because they are held to account for outcomes, they pay attention to how those outcomes are reported. Things have changed as a result of the implementation of the policies. The paperwork has increased because of the need to generate education plans and results reviews. The principal is charged with the responsibility of the report writing, which adds to his administrative duties. At the same time this added responsibility forces him to pay attention to what is going on in classrooms and increases his supervision and instructional leadership duties. This is the double edge of the sword as described by O'Sullivan; more work and added responsibility to account for results on the one side, and improved access to instructional leadership and teachers in classrooms on the other.

O'Sullivan explains how the new reports demand information on completion rates that is difficult to obtain. Adelaide has a very transient school population. Parents in the hospitality industry and in other industries in town are mobile. Completion rates of the grade 9 cohorts are not highly correlated with the grade 12s because the students leave town. "We lose them in the province, to other provinces, to private schools. We are very transient." O'Sullivan admits that it is difficult to report completion rates when he does not have the complete data.

Coaching Conversations

Another change identified by O'Sullivan is a change in the kinds of conversations he is having with teachers and the school council. These conversations, and the discussions with parents at parent-teacher interviews or off-campus, focus on results and test scores more than they have in the past. "I think in that way everybody is aware, or more aware, of the exams and results. They are asking more questions."

Aside from the increased opportunity for conversation and a change in the tone of the conversation, the policy implementation has caused O'Sullivan to think differently about his work as a school administrator. "I guess it makes me more accountable for the overall results, I sort of feel more accountable, and as I feel more accountable, then maybe I put a little more pressure on other people to be accountable." His own accountability or responsibility is transferred to others in a chain of accountability from the province, through the School District to the school, the teachers and the students. Along the chain, behaviour is changing as the new definition and expectations for socially desirable behaviour becomes clear. O'Sullivan explains this transition in terms of more public accountability rather than more public responsibility. He is held to account, and because he is vicariously responsible for the actions of others, he holds others to account for the results on standardized tests.

Leadership: Coaching Techniques

O'Sullivan reports that he believes in moral leadership, "the kind that Thomas Sergiovanni writes about." He expects professionalism from teachers and believes that they do have a moral responsibility, a moral duty. Because of that, they understand the importance of success for students and accountability to students, parents and the community at large. Although he is talking about vicarious responsibility for his teachers, he uses the language of accountability for success and results.

O'Sullivan often ponders how his role has changed. "I guess it has changed the requirements I put on people to give me examples of their accountability—give me a report of 'This is what I think happened or did not happen.'"

Students: The Players

Although O'Sullivan reports a different approach for holding himself to account for student results, his approach to students remains the same. He stresses the importance of diploma exams to the students. He believes that the emphasis on test results has put a lot of pressure on students, too.

I do not think [my approach] has changed. I think I have always talked to students about being successful and working hard and doing as well as you can. I think I put emphasis on diploma exams as well as other kinds of instruction, now and in the past.

This kind of encouragement has always been a part of his interaction with students.

I guess from my own point of view the differences I think about are around the profession and the importance of the fact that the public seems to think that they can hold us to account about the exams...We have been nailed pretty hard by the Fraser Report, which ranks schools according to academic achievement. And no matter how you explain it, it always sounds like you're making an excuse.

When the Fraser Institute started publishing their report, the results would come in and teachers would analyze them for hours at a time. That time did not seem like time well spent to O'Sullivan. He believes that a better way to spend time is on curriculum and ensuring that it is properly covered for the students. That's where he believes teachers should be held to account. O'Sullivan feels time is wasted justifying results rather than planning how to better address the curriculum.

Speaking as an administrator, O'Sullivan compares his school to others and considers that he is fortunate to have staffing numbers that allow class sizes to remain low. Classes are smaller. This may contribute to the success of the students, he admits. Students have more one-on-one time with the teachers. Most of the staff who teach diploma exam subjects have been at Adelaide for 15 to 35 years. These teachers are confident and comfortable with their assessment of how their students will do on the exams. O'Sullivan explains that teacher-awarded marks are usually close to the provincial marks. O'Sullivan is proud of his staff and their experience and competence. He seems to recognize, respect and appreciate their contributions.

Academic Focus: Skills Practice

O'Sullivan talks about the academic focus and how the majority of students enrol in three sciences and Math 31. Some Adelaide students in grade 12 earn 40 credits in their last year and graduate with 125 credits when they need only 100. "We have a strong academic focus." Expectations are that the students will go to post-secondary institutions and that they will learn something in every class. The administrative practices that influence the success of the school in raising grades are difficult for O'Sullivan to identify. Any small school experiences peaks and valleys that are often beyond the school's control. The school might do well for a while, and even though it keeps doing the same things, it could possibly run into difficulty in a certain year. "You do not really know why, whether it is a bad year in numerology or something, but you can really see the difference," he says, sharing his sense of mystery around why one cohort of students is different from the next.

He goes on to explain that in small schools it is possible that in some cohorts the grade 12s are strong academically and other years they are not. "That is why we really have to be careful that we are not looking at, or reacting too much to one set of exams, gloating too much or looking for reasons. Because the next year, or two years down the road, things can change." Overreacting or early congratulations are dangerous in this situation, according to O'Sullivan. He reports that it is better to look at results over the long run and to identify patterns than to focus on one group of students. As coach, O'Sullivan knows that a championship team can still have a year where talent is scarce or over-concentrated. In sports, as well, long-term achievement is the real test of a good coach.

Pride and Contribution

O'Sullivan explains that at Adelaide the students are encouraged to take ownership for their learning. Classes are not scheduled every day. Work blocks are scheduled with the teacher twice a week and then the students are expected to put in three hours a week on their own. That time can be during school hours or after. If students work on subjects during the day, they can access a teacher if they have questions. With this kind of scheduling in place students can work together using peer-coaching to learn from each other as well as from the face-to-face classes with the teachers. "I do not know if that has any correlation with anything, but it could," admits O'Sullivan.

Usually the school has a testing centre in operation. The centre allows students flexibility and choice as to when they write unit exams and other tests. Students can determine for themselves when they are ready for unit exams and other tests and write them at their own discretion. One student might write an exam on a Thursday but another can go to the teacher and negotiate more time and not write until Tuesday. Exams are modified at the testing center in these cases.

The idea behind the testing centre is that students write exams when they feel prepared. This concept recognizes the different learning styles and pace of learning that each student has. O'Sullivan suggests that Adelaide students are better prepared when they are writing exams, so their school-awarded marks improve and their preparedness for the diploma has improved. At the very least, he adds, students have become accustomed to making decisions on how prepared they are for an exam. They have the experience of being prepared for an exam and know what "being prepared" feels like.

O'Sullivan reports that students are anxious to write exams after the study units are complete because they want to get on with the next unit. They do not like having an exam hanging over their heads while the class moves on. Students can schedule their readiness for exams in their day timers. O'Sullivan explains that they are learning to be responsible for their own learning, which he feels is having an impact on results.

This ownership among students for their own readiness to write exams seems comparable to what happens at the Gardener's St. Lawrence High School. Reassessment is used there in a similar way to allow students to determine their own sense of preparedness for exams. This flexibility to determine readiness seems to foster a greater degree of success on exams and develops in students the habit of being successful on exams. At St. Lawrence and at Adelaide, success on school based exams is breeding success on provincial standardized tests.

Other factors that influence the upswing in the results at Adelaide include what O'Sullivan describes as normal, standard fare at high schools across the province. Test banks and practice exams in class are all a part of the routine of preparation for school and diploma exams.

Special seminars are held at Adelaide with a focus on preparation for the exams. These seminars are not directly aimed at preparing students to actually write a particular exam. They are question and answer sessions that explore 1) the *types* of questions that would probably appear on a given test; 2) some general exam writing strategies; 3) the kinds of questions that go with graphs; and 4) other exam writing topics. These seminars take place after regular school hours and during school. Some are held on weekends. One teacher invites her small class of eight students to meet at her house. This kind of commitment and connectedness adds to the teacher's credibility and to a sense of the expectations the teacher holds for herself and her students.

Defensive Coaching for Offensive Strength

At Adelaide, strong academics are linked to other strong programs in the school related to the arts or to sports. Of the 100 students who are residents of Adelaide, O'Sullivan reports that 40 are members of the school band. Adelaide has a strong band program and a strong athletics program, given the size of the school. Along with the 100 resident students, there are about 20 to 25 American students who come to Adelaide to attend hockey school. The Adelaide Hockey Camp students attend a half-day of classes and go to hockey practice for the other half-day. Most of them return to the United States to graduate. The ones who do graduate from Adelaide do very well in academic achievement, even though they have not been exposed to the provincial curriculum all the way along. One important contribution that these students make is a financial one. These students are assessed foreign student fees that go directly into the Adelaide Community High School budget, rather than into the school division's general budget. This provides financial flexibility for Adelaide that is not experienced in many other schools in the province.

A number of students are involved in drama, even though the school does not have a formal program. The school has a good relationship with the community, perhaps a carry-over from the community school charter days. A community parent works with the drama students. O'Sullivan mentions that there are high school credits available for programs like that, but so far Adelaide has not granted these students credits. Students have not requested those credits, so there has been no need to consider that.

Like most schools in the province, Adelaide has a core group of students who are involved in everything. They are taking a full load of courses in the academic stream. They are involved in the band. They play on one or two of the sports teams, and they earn good grades. These are the ultimate targets of O'Sullivan's teaching team.

Parental Support

According to O'Sullivan, changes in accountability policy have focused the parents on the exam results, "especially when you get to grade 12". Parents boycotted the achievement exams at grade 9 in his school. They did not, however, boycott the diploma exams. O'Sullivan thinks that teachers ought to be held more and more accountable by the parents. At the same time he believes that every student should have the opportunity to be successful in a course. By his own admission, he would not ever want to get to the point where educators are screening students for entrance to a course or counselling students not to write the exam because of the possibility they might not do well. Each student has the right to at least attempt the exam, according to O'Sullivan.

Parents are becoming more aware of the exam "game" and O'Sullivan has noticed that the students are also more aware. They are challenging teachers more about the marks and are anxious to earn diplomas. O'Sullivan reports that students are very aware of how important marks are and that the marks they earn in class translate to school-based marks, which represent

50 percent of their final grade. Students definitely want to keep their marks high. It is risky for them to put all of their hopes on the two-hour exam. Those two hours can change their life. Which doors open or close on their future depend on how they do in the two hours, averaged with the mark assigned to them by the school.

Except for the fact that people are calling educators more to account for what happens in schools, O'Sullivan is convinced that not much has changed in practice over the time he has spent in high schools. He believes that some of the long-established practices of administrators and teachers, such as the analysis of exams, have now been justified by the new emphasis on accountability. He does not necessarily agree with the public ranking of schools that the Fraser Institute is known to do. He tells of picking up a magazine published by an elite private school that has always placed first or second in the Frasier rankings. This private school's own magazine describes the ranking in the *Fraser Institute Report Card on High Schools* as "unfair" and O'Sullivan agrees.

O'Sullivan is firmly on the accountability side of the conversation in his move toward desirable behaviour. He has been held to account and in turn holds others to account. The success of the school, his staff and his students is a measure of how he manages to focus attention on the scores and to negotiate perceptions of their importance or their level of priority for the school stake holders.

O'Sullivan, as Coach, sets the goals and supports skill development to achieve the goals. He expects his teaching staff to understand what is necessary to build a championship team and then to do it. This approach has created an environment at Adelaide that allows the well-qualified staff team to teach its students to achieve measurable improvement in academic achievement as measured by exam results.

It is the end of the season. The final game has played out on the field, a field littered with the detritus of celebration for a game well played. Win or lose the coach quietly follows his team off the field knowing that they have achieved the maximum result, given the particular circumstances of the season. This kind of sustained achievement, built over iterations of many seasons past, brings perhaps the highest satisfaction and recognition the person behind the bench can receive.

Characteristics of the Coach:
- Goal oriented
- Informal
- Focused
- Mature
- Aware
- Team-focused
- Steady
- Calm

To be effective the Coach Leader needs to:
- Accept the role as a leader who works through others
- Identify work that is both strategic and uniquely his or hers
- Delegate
- Recruit staff with complementary skills
- Spend time mentoring others

To work with a Coach others need to:
- Be open to coaching for performance
- Be willing to acknowledge performance gaps and opportunities
- Be able to set realistic goals to close performance gaps and exploit opportunities

Chapter 5: The Rescuer

Dunbrach Catholic Junior and Senior High School

The Rescuer serves as our guide through our journeys of transition that result from the changes imposed by crisis. Decisions and situations that call for a response can incite change quickly, but human transitions, the adaptation to change, take time. People in organizational transition imposed by poor performance or external pressures may still want to conserve the old way. They "resist", finding it hard to let go of old paradigms, especially when the changes threaten roles and even identities. This is natural in social systems, which seek to remain stable, even when the dynamic stability may be problematic. It is the wise leader, indeed, who can lead transitions from behind, supporting, guiding and assisting people across the long and often chaotic bridge that takes us from the present into the future.

In this sense the Rescuer, sent in to "turn the school around" views his staff as the "heroes" and himself as a "servant" who can guide and assist them through their own transformational journeys. Rather than continually deferring to the direction of his reports, the Rescuer must weigh their perspective and experience as he makes decisions guided by his own professional judgement. The Rescuer uses his own strong and imposing professional will to move the organization to its desired future.

William Johnson, the principal of Dunbrach Catholic High School, sees himself as a rescuer. From his perspective, education is a crisis and he is managing the situation so as to minimize damage and rescue the school and its people. He identifies himself as one of the "crisis managers" for the School District. "Anytime there is a problem in a school—it needs to be closed, it needs to amalgamate, the school being in crisis, out of control, whatever—I am the one that is sent." He admits that he was sent to turn Dunbrach around and that there was incredible tension; it was a difficult place for adults before he came.

Johnson is an experienced high school administrator who came from a Physical Education background. Even as he approaches eligibility for retirement, he is obviously strong and athletic. He has a wonderful smile that transforms to a gentle frown of concern when he talks of serious things. His demeanour ensures visitors feel relaxed and at home with him and in his school. His kind, gentle exterior belies the strength he shows to anyone or any organization posing a threat to people in his charge. He still has a competitive edge that motivates him and those around him to be the best they can be.

Dunbrach is unique as the only school catering to both senior and junior high school students in the School District. The Dunbrach school building still has the split entrance that it had when the junior and senior high programs were run separately and the school had two names. It is a sprawling low, brown building that is unmistakably a school. This is the typical school of the 1970s that has stood the test of time. It is clean and comfortable even in its institutionalism. At the entrance, the prerequisite trophy case greets visitors with trophies that have accumulated many additions to their original bases over the years, still proudly displayed and presumably coveted. The main office, denoted only by a small overhead sign, is several left and right turns and a half kilometre walk away. Young, shy junior school girls offer amused and shy guidance to stray visitors, leading the way down the four different halls through a section of the school they rarely venture into, savouring glimpses of senior school boys.

The Firefighter

Johnson believes that the school is only as good as the staff he works with, and that everyone chipping in the way they do improves the tone of the school. "If William Johnson looks good in

Dunbrach, or anybody here looks good, it is because administration and teachers do their job," he announces proudly. His presence and visibility in the school contributes to his relationship with teachers. Johnson, in his role as Rescuer, is interested in gaining the trust of his staff. One of the ways he has set out to do that is to live among them and walk the talk. Johnson explains that all members of the administration team have teaching responsibilities. They feel it is important to be able to set an example for the teachers. Principal Johnson explains, "I have always said for me to go in and evaluate teachers and not have been in a class for 15 years is ludicrous, because there is no doubt that the job has changed dramatically." The teachers appreciate the presence of the team in the classroom, according to Johnson. He believes that it adds to their respect for the team. It also adds to the team's credibility because they are willing to be held to account by others, as well as holding others to account. It creates a sense of shared history between the teachers and the administrative staff. The proximity of the administrative team and the clarity of expectation through modeling in the classroom contribute to the sense of how significant the leader is in the life of the follower.

Principal Johnson shows a genuine respect and appreciation for the work of his staff. Teachers are given time in lieu for evening meetings. He always gives time in lieu on a Friday afternoon so as to extend their weekend. He recognizes that with collective agreements, he is limited to how he can reward teachers for extra efforts, but he does as much as he can to show his gratitude for their commitment to the success of the students. Johnson is also quick to give credit where credit is due, as he puts it, to the teachers. "I am the least important person in the building," he admits. This is not to say that he feels that the contribution he makes as the principal is unimportant. He explains that he feels strongly that he adds great value to the school community, but it is the teachers who are in front of the students every day, day in, day out. His appreciation for the work of the teachers is clearly stated.

Shift Change

Johnson reports that he is the third principal to have "ruled" Dunbrach in three years, and three of four administrators at Dunbrach are new this year. He gives credit to the staff for having maintained the reputation and success of the school over that time. Each new team of principals and vice-principals brings with it different philosophies and expectations. Johnson refers to the staff as a "very, very hardy bunch." In the absence of immediate and approximate accountability because of an administration in flux, the continued success of staff and students increasing test scores could be attributed to a high degree of responsibility and personal commitment among staff members. This suggests that maybe, as long as principals are doing no harm, teachers can manage the continuous improvement themselves.

Johnson explains that Dunbrach has always been a training ground for administrators, especially assistant principals. It is a place where assistant principals get a quick on-the-job lesson because of the demands of grades 7-12 junior/senior high school programs. The dual program also prepares them for the administrative positions at the school board office. Again, this uniqueness contributes to the sense of responsibility of the administrators, who report that the opportunity to work at Dunbrach affords further opportunities or rewards in the future.

Johnson notes that there has been staff turnover as well. Conflicts with administration sent some staff looking for other positions within the district before the change in administration was announced. Does the conflict with administration strengthen the resolve of the staff to do well? Johnson believes that change is healthy. He, himself, has never been at a school for more than two years. Speaking philosophically about his role as "clean-up guy," he admits that it is not as difficult as people might think. "I

> *Working to improve academic results is the number one thing I can do as an administrator.*
>
> Rich O'Sullivan, Coach

said that it is the easiest job in the world as far as I am concerned because you go in and it does not take a lot (to make a positive difference)." Johnson explains that teachers,by their nature, do not expect big changes. A new principal needs only to pay attention to the little things and to stay out of their way. Teachers will do their job and they know what their job is. He believes that if he supports teachers, they will willingly and gladly step up to the plate to do what they need to do for students.

Johnson describes his own style as a "What can I do to help you?" style, a big change from the dictatorial style of his predecessor. He reports that the door is never closed in the office. Teachers are encouraged not to close classroom doors except out of consideration for others if there is noise. This open-door policy is what Markum, the Impresario, fought to achieve at Rosedale. There is a common belief that open doors seem to lead to a more collaborative, more supportive environment. Both principals report that the staff are very appreciative of these efforts to increase visibility.

Sharing the Glory

There is also a leadership team in the school, that has been in place since before Johnson came, who vet ideas before they are brought to the general staff or to the grade level or department meetings. Things such as the school growth plans, crisis-management plans, and other long-range planning documents required by the School District first go to the leadership team for input and review. Much of the documentation is written by Johnson and then brought to the group. "In those cases they asked if I would do them. They said 'We do not want to sit for 50 or 60 hours doing this. Will you write it and bring it to us?' So I said sure. So I have done all of those myself. They have all been approved." Johnson sees this task as a way to relieve teachers of some of the "administration" that might otherwise burden them "because the bottom line is they have to teach in class and that is where I want them to do their work". This attitude is shared by Norquay the Sherpa.

Johnson talks more about site-based decision making and his understanding of teachers' attitudes.

They (teachers) do not really want to be involved in all those decisions. They want to know what they have to teach, when they have to teach it, when their spare is, when their holidays are, etc., and the rest of the stuff 'you guys can take care of for us'.

Once documents are prepared or plans made, the staff is invited to peruse, question and challenge anything. What they think needs changing is revisited. Johnson's contribution is time. By taking care of the planning aspect he is able to focus teacher activity in the classroom and provide a service to teachers. He believes that teachers appreciate the time it takes to generate the plans and that they seem happy to leave that to someone who is not burdened with the duty of care that comes with classroom responsibility. They provide valuable input, they review and comment, but the work of creating the documentation falls to Johnson. This is one way for him to negotiate the perceptions that staff have of him as leader.

To the Rescue

Johnson is at the school each morning very early. He spends quiet time in the morning writing the reports for staff approval. As Rescuer, he sees the crisis management plan as necessary and valuable and admits that before he came to the school there was no crisis management plan. The school growth plan is also something that he created himself and that was later approved and adjusted by the staff. The process of providing growth plans and required documentation to the province appears to have little importance or value to him; he seems nonchalant about it. This is a revelation for those who still see these as vital, essential documents. Norquay the Sherpa might be awed and liberated by Johnson's perception of the requirements. The Sherpa might say,

You mean there is another way to create plans? You mean you do not have to drag staff kicking and screaming through endless meetings to end up where you were last year, identifying the same goals with renewed commitment? You mean I can write them myself? WOW!

This underlines the importance of the interpretation from the leadership to the followership on issues of accountability and responsibility. From the superintendent, through the principal, to the staff, interpretations will change perceptions of the control, priority and expectations of behaviour. Layers of leadership influence the perception of accountability and responsibility within each School District.

Maintain Open Communication

Another focus for Dunbrach, Johnson admits, is a change to a more collegial and more positive environment amongst the staff. "That has occurred," reports Johnson. As evidence, he notes that there are a lot more people in a staffroom that had been pretty much empty prior to his arrival. The school projects a sense of friendliness, confidence, of open classroom doors, and curiosity about a stranger with no fear or suspicion. They seem comfortable.

Coming back to the reports, he admits that they have to be dealt with. "Of course you have to put all the numbers in, and the test results, and all of the other kinds of things that are all part of that," he says, making it sound easy. "Once that is done we meet; I meet with Joe, the superintendent, and the admin team." He admits that he does not have to include the administrative team in these conversations but he prefers that they are there. "We go over our results, our enrolment, trends, our growth plan, and last year's growth plan. Were we successful, what worked and what did not work?" He also gives substitute coverage so that the staff members have a chance to sit down with the superintendent to ask him any questions of interest to them, whether they be school related, district related, contractual—any subject of their choice. He identifies this visit by the superintendent as a chance for staff to rub shoulders with him, a rare opportunity in a School District of this size.

> *I provide lunch for them that day and so on, so it is a chance to sit back and they enjoy it because we have representation not just from teachers, custodial had representation there, support staff have, the secretary is there, not to take notes but on behalf of the office staff which she oversees for me, to ask questions or bring any information back.*

This opportunity to visit with the superintendent is new to the school since Johnson joined the staff. The previous administration had a different, less inclusive approach to growth plans and central office personnel availability. Johnson lets staff know that they can even ask about him when they talk to the superintendent. He does not attend the meeting with the staff so that they will feel free to say whatever needs saying. He does not ask staff about the meeting afterwards, either. He is proud of this gift he gives to his staff. He adds, "Joe comes back and thanks me. Obviously, he enjoys them."

Johnson encourages staff to let him know if he has "screwed up or messed up". He says that if he has a problem with one of the staff, he lets him or her know, and he expects the same kind of treatment in return. Open and honest communication is important to him. That open and honest approach is also applied to the students in the school. Johnson explains that students are welcome in the office, and they come in to tell good stories as well as to share problems. Johnson reports a concerted effort by the administrative team to change the image of the front office to one of caring concern rather than a fearful place where no one wants to go. For Johnson, relationship building seems to be a major focus. This is understandable given his position as the new administration—the rescuer—in a school that he feels has been wounded by events of the past.

Proud Parent: Vested Rescuer

Principal Johnson is a resident of the neighbourhood and a parent at the school. Describing the community as a "very, very middle class, upper class area", he explains that what that means for him is that people make assumptions, some erroneous, about the kind of students who attend the school and the kind of programs and administration that are needed. Johnson relates how living in the community gives him the insider information on what people in the community, the parents of the students, are really like, "... and now I wear a hat and glasses to go to Safeway just so that I do not get accosted. I joke I cannot go and sit on the park bench and drink any more now that they know who I am." He is very aware of the expectation in this neighbourhood though he says that it has not been a problem being a parent, a resident, and the local high school principal. "They are very, very demanding." The parents are professionals and expect their children to achieve at a certain level.

For some students the high expectations pose a problem because they do not have that ability. "They are not going to be brain surgeons. That is a reality. Try and let a parent understand that." Johnson says that it is especially difficult for parents of students who live in the neighbourhood to accept this reality because the perception is that the people who live in this community are all brain surgeons, doctors, lawyers, teachers and engineers. Nevertheless, not all of their children are capable of reaching the standards set by the parents, and helping these exceptional parents accept that reality is sometimes difficult.

Johnson's role as community member and parent may add a different dimension to the transparency and openness that he practises and expects. It seems to influence teachers' perceptions of him, and his appreciation of them. It also seems to influence his credibility among the teachers and the parents and to bring him closer to the classroom as a client as well as a supervisor. It gives him a valuable perspective on all aspects of the school and its community. His role as parent seems to add to his credibility, his recognition, and proximity to this community. Do the teachers understand that the person who is judging them has three perspectives, that of parent, colleague, and leader? The affluence of the community is undeniable, and the district and school websites confirm the uniqueness of the school within the district, but what is the significance of Johnson's uniqueness as an administrator, community member and parent?

The Rescue Team

Demanding parents can sometimes influence the kind of teacher that is attracted to a school. The school has more very young staff, especially at the junior high level, than many other schools. Johnson describes the staff, as a whole, as core subject specialists, except for those who have arrived from other schools after being declared redundant. "They were put here without any interview or anything else. They have taught the subject, but I am going to be honest...if I get to declare someone redundant I am going to look at my weakest teacher in that subject area to declare redundant. That is a reality". By this statement he insinuates that those teachers who were declared redundant by other principals and ended up on his staff are there because they were the weakest teachers in that subject area. Because of contracts and the collective agreement, these teachers' jobs are protected, so that if there is a decrease in population in one school, then other schools are expected to find room for them even though they may not be the best teachers for the positions. Johnson feels that this really is a "no win" situation where the surplus teacher is unhappy and the staff forced to accept him or her is unhappy. Johnson is philosophical about it when he says, "So that is a constant battle that we face."

Johnson recognizes that as a result of this highly motivated student population, a number of staff members are "resting on their laurels". He explains, "We challenge them to get involved with the assessment for learning, which in this school is a dirty word. It is in most high schools." The teachers have risen to the challenge, and to their credit they have become involved in the assessment-for-learning program. The program is a standing session that is scheduled at general staff meetings. "We study vignettes and throw out some ideas and some different scenarios and bang those around." For example, a teacher asks a question at one of these sessions, "When do I give a student a zero for late assignments?" Johnson answers with another question, "Are you marking the assignment or are you marking the behaviour?" He reframes the question and puts it to the teacher another way. "The Teacher's Association says you are supposed to be here 15 minutes before the bell goes, but when you walk in late do I dock you pay? Am I paying you for what you are doing in the classroom in essence, or am I paying you for your behaviour?" With these questions, Johnson has demonstrated his willingness to hold his staff members publicly accountable when their behaviour does not conform to his expectations. He does so as gently as he can, but he remains committed to a single set of standards for students and teachers. The reality, of course, is that Johnson does not pay the teachers. The school jurisdiction does. Everyone understands that a principal does not have the power to withhold pay, but the point is made. The point is that students should be assessed on what they are learning rather than on how they were behaving. Johnson advocates for students and he is not tolerant of teachers who have different standards for their own behaviour than they have for the behaviour of students in their care.

Women and Children First

Johnson's passion for a successful rescue shows as he talks about the chemistry class. Chemistry results on the standardized test scores are very weak compared to physics and biology. This is particularly troublesome for Johnson when he considers that many of the students are looking at careers related to the sciences; engineering, math and other science and related professions. Johnson wants desperately to the right thing, but discretion is necessary when dealing with someone in the same professional association. Sometimes the right thing means to take sides with the students. Clearly, there is an expectation that students will perform on the exams at a certain level. Below that expectation there are consequences for teachers. As an avowed students' advocate, Johnson struggles with what is going on with students in the class:

> *Coming in here was a huge task in my own mind because of what is going on here. Yet you have a person and a personality here who believes he or she knows more than anyone else around. And they do know chemistry. Gosh they know chemistry as much or better than anyone I have ever seen.*

Subject expertise is not a problem in this classroom. "But as I said earlier, knowing and teaching are two different entities." Johnson states that he has a clear expectation that being able to teach the subject in an effective way, as measured by results, is very important.

Johnson spoke with the teacher and posed the difficult questions, "Why are you teaching? Why are you doing this?" He was surprised to learn the teacher planned to work toward a position in administration. Johnson suggested that becoming an administrator requires a level of teaching expertise that other teachers respect. Johnson was very honest with the teacher, and he did contact the superintendent about his concerns. He let the teacher know by telling him, "I know you are in line for an appointment. You will not receive one until I say yes. Because I will not do that to the staff, and we cannot keep doing this to the students." He influenced or negotiated the teacher's perceptions of the external situation and increased the teacher's understanding of the significance of the event. He reports that the individual started to work at becoming a better teacher but accepted the responsibility reluctantly. For this teacher, it is a matter of accepting that there is more to learn. Johnson has provided fair and firm treatment of this teacher, according to the teacher's comments.

It seems that Johnson's advice comes not from being a chemistry expert but from being a caring advocate for students. Most of the time, he feels there is room to compromise when working with staff, but in this instance it became evident from the data that something had to change. His respect for the teacher is evident as he relates his attempt to help the teacher improve, to identify what administration's expectations are, and to provide some candid feedback.

Keeping in Shape

Johnson identifies the connection between improving test scores and leadership practices as being visible and available to staff and students. "They know who we are. They know we are here to support them." Johnson believes that by the time an administrator enters a teacher's classroom to do an evaluation of the teaching, the administrator ought to be known to the teachers and the students. "If you have not been in their class before, you are not getting a real sense of the class. So students need to be comfortable with me wandering in and sitting down." Johnson is known to step into a classroom just to share a joke with a teacher. The purpose of the visit might be to lighten things up in the middle of some deep lesson, after a teacher has had a tough night with a new baby, or just to break the tension and allow everyone to relax, at least for a moment. There are teachers who might not be as appreciative as others of what they might refer to as an intrusion.

As Johnson states, visibility is important but teachers can be guarded and territorial about their space. "We just go in and sit down with the students when they are doing a group project and just become another person in the room." These kinds of visits afford Johnson the "legitimate" feel for what is going on that he is looking for. He believes that he can get that feeling only when it is clear that he is not coming in to evaluate. Being visible and having the staff comfortable with him are important to Johnson. He is also vigilant in his "raising the bar" activities with teachers. "I expect more of them than they have ever given in their life," he explains. He expects staff to work hard and to play hard. Those expectations are explicit, and he supports them by providing teachers with time and money for their own professional improvement. Johnson himself is not one to sit still or to spend days twiddling his thumbs. He jokes, "I tell teachers 'You think I am working so hard in the office. I just close the blinds. I am actually having a sleep'."

Building Community

If staff members are dissatisfied with what is going on they are always invited to share their concerns with Johnson. He has made it okay for staff to come in and ask "*Why?*" "I am so far from perfect, it is frightening," he jokes. He is quick to tell students in trouble that he has sat in the same chair. "I was rotten in high school," he adds. He recounts that some of the things he did in high school would have meant a suspension or maybe an expulsion today. He does not kid himself or others about being "up for sainthood." He respects the fact that teachers make mistakes. "We had a case this week where I had to suspend a teacher. It needed to be done." The teacher was having problems and Johnson believed that it was in the best interest of the teacher to give a suspension. He reports that the other members of staff came up afterward and thanked him for doing what he felt he had to do. "Because it really showed that I cared about the teacher. I do not want the teacher to lose a career or anything else, but the teacher needs some help." The staff appreciates the fact that Johnson is willing to step up to the plate and do what has to be done. Johnson's philosophical approach is that "we are only as good as all of us."

William Johnson really is "one of the gang". He explains how others see his role,

> I have the title and I still chuckle because when I got my first pay cheque here someone says 'Can I see your pay stub?' I said 'sure.' No big deal, figure out what I get, it is not like it is a secret what I get paid. And he looked at me and says, 'Are you an idiot?' I said 'What do you mean?' He says 'You do everything you do for that little bit of money?' He says 'I am not going into administration. Obviously, you do not get paid enough'.

Johnson does not complain. In his opinion he makes a decent salary. The comment by the friend also indicates a respect for the work that Johnson is doing, and for him that recognition is more important than the pay cheque. What motivates Johnson is creating a culture, a friendly, productive atmosphere where students can learn. "I meet every day with the support staff and have coffee because they are a huge part of it. I come in once or twice a week at night to visit with the custodian and see how things are going there." His commitment is evident to everyone—management by walking around, by dealing with things as they arise, by building relationships before the problem arises, and by appreciating everyone's efforts.

Johnson understands the importance of support and custodial staff in the fabric of the school's culture, and he includes them so that everyone on staff sees the "whole" rather than the parts.

> Anytime we do anything in the building it is as a whole (staff). So when we gave teachers an afternoon off for the parent-teacher interviews, all support staff, custodian, got the afternoon as well. So we try and do it across board because, as I said, we are all part of the whole picture.

He is responsible for contracts with the staff in the cafeteria, and although he does not pay the custodial staff members, they report to him. Maintenance is a district responsibility but he still likes to maintain good relationships with those who work on his building. This is not to take away from the importance of teaching, which he identifies as primary. He explains that he understands that without the other parts of the whole, the teaching cannot occur. He sees, as Norquay the Sherpa has, that it is his responsibility to manage the non-teaching aspects so that the teaching and the teachers are unencumbered.

Johnson, the Rescuer, seems to have moved Dunbrach towards his goal of a friendlier place. His mission is to create an improved atmosphere for the adults in the building. He seems to be successfully negotiating perceptions with staff so that, whether through responsibility or accountability, teachers are moving toward activities in classrooms that may or may not translate into increased test scores. Teachers seem to be key to success in this school, where administrative turnover makes inquiring into leadership practices tricky. Despite the turmoil, the staff manages to provide opportunities for student results to continue to rise. Aside from resourceful parents and students, and teachers concerned with maintaining academic success, Johnson is not able to identify the leadership practices that have contributed to the increased test scores.

The Rescuer, despite popular misconceptions, has not led a charge through his organization on a white horse, flags flying. Rather, through small incremental changes in attitude, structure, processes, and through modeling behaviour, he builds a community of trust and relationship that has the ship moving steadily in the right direction. The Rescuer allows his quiet presence to impact the organization and its culture. The Rescuer, having set a transition in motion, never entirely certain of the outcome, will always be prepared to move on to the next assignment.

Characteristics of the Rescuer:
- Courageous
- Supporting
- Modeling
- Humble
- Strong willed
- Empathetic
- Trusting
- Trustworthy

To be effective a Rescuer needs to:
- Seek a challenge
- Seek new and novel contexts
- Create pressure for change
- Seek opportunities for innovation
- Work with people he or she can respect

To work with a Rescuer, others need to:
- Be open to change and innovation
- Be ready to go with the flow
- Work for improvement
- Recognize if they are seen as an obstacle to change

Chapter 6: The Gardener

St Lawrence High School

The technology and the fertilizer may have changed, but over the millennia the Gardener has approached the task of coaxing the best out of the earth in much the same way. First, the most suitable and most fertile patch of ground is found. The proper time is selected during which to plant: a certain season, a certain phase of the moon, after a special ritual. Plants or seeds are selected and placed where they will thrive, perhaps in dryer or wetter soil, perhaps in the shade or in the sunlight. The growing plants are carefully nourished with nutrients and water. Weeds are removed before they displace or strangle the desired vegetation. The Gardener carefully nourishes now for the richer harvest later, managing the vagaries of nature—including the weather and pestilence—reaps the harvest at the end of each season and begins again.

The mission of the school reads, "We will help every student achieve success within a Catholic Faith Community." The tenets and the methods used to accomplish the mission are listed in the operational plan. The commitments and the tenets contribute to the fertile ground for learning represented by St. Lawrence High School. There is an expectation that the potential of each individual student will be nurtured and cultivated if the tenets and commitments are honoured.

The principal, Matthew Hunter, returns to the tenets and pillars again and again. He demonstrates a commitment to the spirit of the mission as well as to the language of the principles described in the operational plan. According to Hunter, there seems to be no confusion about identity and purpose for the staff. St. Lawrence is a school firmly grounded and purposeful. The building is new and the school's partnership with the adjacent YMCA is important for the community and for the students of the school. The fitness facilities are accessible to students and afford them an opportunity to mix with other members of the neighbourhood on a regular basis in a positive, collegial, supportive and nurturing atmosphere.

The school is bright and clean, full of students who are smiling and joking with one another in a friendly, caring manner. They seem to notice visitors but there is no real acknowledgement as they continue on their way to and from class, armed with backpacks and gym bags. St Lawrence High School is a school that has shown increasing average test results over a period of three years. This is the principal's story.

The Garden

Matthew Hunter is a tall man sporting the long nails of a classical guitarist on only one hand. He has a beard and a quiet, soft demeanour, which makes a visitor feel at home right away. Although test scores have improved over the past there years, Hunter does not concede that test score results are the focus. For Hunter, the focus is students and their success. One measure of that success, and only one, is scores. There are many other objective and subjective factors included in measures of success at St. Lawrence. The school has identified pillars such as outcome-based education. The pillars are included in the operational plan of the school. Hunter reads them from a poster on the wall:

1. Catholicity
2. Academic Programming
3. Outcomes-Based, Mastery Learning
4. Assessment to reflect Outcomes-based learning
5. Teacher as TA, Instructor and Team Planner
6. Added meaning through long blocks, overlap and hands-on
7. The College System with teams of teachers/staff

Because of the emphasis on the outcomes-based approach, planning, in-servicing, and professional development are focused on learning more about the outcome-based model where students can experience success. The curriculum is delivered and assessed with the aim of having students achieve mastery. Hunter's idea is that planning and delivering curriculum with all of the students' learning in mind focuses everyone's attention on learning. Further, he feels that it is the focus on learning, on growth, that has become the driver in this particular building, not the scores on standardized tests. Modalities such as visual, auditory, kinesthetic and others, explain the uniqueness of each individual and his or her learning needs. According to Hunter, these are contributing factors for the kind of success that St. Lawrence has established in its standardized test results.

> *Like plants growing toward the light, students are attracted to success by being successful.*
>
> Matthew Hunter, Gardener

A focus on quality and success for individual students has resulted in a better educational experience and overall improvement in test scores. Hunter explains that the staff and students are continually trying to improve their showing in the standard of excellence, having achieved an enhanced showing in the acceptable standard category. Hunter admits that they are sometimes below the provincial average for the number of students who meet the standard of excellence, but considering the heterogeneous multicultural population and the area of the city where the school is situated, he feels they are doing as well as can be expected. Hunter has negotiated a perception among the staff and students that the school is unique. By deemphasizing the importance of the test scores as a driver for improvement, Hunter has created a situation for teachers where they are encouraged and motivated by the unique situation and have accepted responsibility for the academic growth of the students in their charge.

Garden Plots

The Teacher Advisory, or TA system, was adopted along with the college system when the school was opened. Hunter expects that TAs are on top of any situation that involves the students assigned to them. That includes, but is not limited to, issues of attendance, academic assignments, academic completion, as well as establishment of a plan for completion and communicating the plan to parents. Students and TAs share responsibilities, and for whatever situation students find themselves facing, TAs serve as their first line of contact.

Hunter sees the TA program as having an impact on the increasing test scores. He believes that if you maintain a level of communication about progress with all the stakeholders engaged in a student's education, the result is increased learning measured by better scores. The TA program provides the consistent care and attention that the plants in this garden require in order to bloom and reach their full potential. The valuable connections between students and their TAs and other members of their colleges ensure that students do not slip through the cracks. Students are accountable for their own learning, but at the same time, someone is monitoring their progress, weeding and culling extraneous information and providing water (information) and sunshine (encouragement) for growth. As a result, the students—the plants—flourish.

The TA system is aimed at giving students identity and a sense of belonging. According to Hunter, St. Lawrence High School is committed to respecting the worth and dignity of each of the students. One of the ways used to achieve this goal is to ensure that each student is known personally by a teacher in the school. This is one of the pillars outlined in the operational plan; to that end teachers are charged with a cross-graded group of students that are their teacher advisor or TA group. The teacher is expected to advocate for these students. Hunter reports that over a three-year period they come to know the students well. Teacher advisors are engaged in individual student's graduation plans and are charged with the responsibility of communicating information to parents. This means talking about pre-requisite courses and about the kinds of courses their child should be taking based upon the child's achievement levels, and linking all of that into career planning for the students. According to Hunter and to the school's home page, this structure allows for students to be held to account or to develop a sense of responsibility through clear expectations: a sense of belonging to a smaller group, a sense of being unique and of having control over their own situations.

Hunter explains that TAs meet with students daily. These meetings are usually aimed at taking attendance, checking in, homeroom activities, messages and announcements. They also meet with their cross-graded groups of 18-20 students once a week for one academic period, which is set aside in the schedule for TA activity. During the weekly session, TAs conduct interviews with students about academics, social issues, developmental issues and career planning. TAs do inventories to help students understand their learning styles. They provide lessons in communication skills, study skills and skills for writing reference letters. Students use that time period to engage in conversation with the career practitioner so they can gain an understanding or develop an idea of what they want to do. They are then given an opportunity to directly link their career aspirations to the courses they are taking. Hunter believes that, in most cases, paying attention to individuals, rather than to skills and opportunities, accounts for the success of the TA system. The Hawthorn effect, the Pygmalion effect, and the Anticipatory Principle are at work. All support the fact that growth occurs where attention is focused.

Planning the Garden

The intention around the connection with at least one adult extends into the community with the parents. The college system is a school within a school concept that allows for smaller garden patches or groups of students. Each student, teacher, non-instructional staff member and support staff member is assigned to a college. Colleges have somewhere between 250 and 300 students and TA groups consist of between 18 and 23 students. "We try to keep it somewhat manageable," says Hunter. "We want the students to be able to identify with at least one adult in the building on a regular basis and in a comfortable way." The structure creates a situation where those who hold students to account, the Teacher Advisors, are in close proximity and significant to the students. The individual connection and attention leads to growth of individual students and better overall outcomes. Hunter, by negotiating the expectations of the opportunities presented in the smaller college groupings, is able to instil a sense of responsibility that may not otherwise be present. Well tended plants flourish. Well tended students do too.

The invitation to high levels of parental involvement is evident on the school website, which encourages parents to stay in touch with students about academic progress. Parents are also divided into colleges. The school is careful to keep siblings in the same college. The school includes parents regularly in the activities of the colleges. Hunter expects the TAs to be the first line of communication with parents. If parents have any questions about anything, it is the TA they call. According to Hunter, if the TA is not able to provide a response, then the TA says, "This is where I can go to get the information for you." Staff members conduct interviews based on the TA structure. "We do not have parents speak to subject teachers," explains Hunter, "because the expectation of the TA is to know what is going on for each student."

Parents are asked to come in and get the report cards. "We do not mail the report cards out. We ask the parents, well we demand that the parents come in," admits Hunter. Hunter's firm commitment to his clear expectations leaves no room for confusion about his motives. He explains to parents,

> *We need you to be here. We need you to be part of the process. We need you to be part of the dialogue. So that way, when you receive a report card you are not receiving it in isolation but you are receiving it in a manner where you can collaborate over what is going on and what needs to happen next.*

Teachers have opportunities in the parent-teacher interview log sheets to do goal setting with the parents. They report on next steps for the student. Next steps might be developmental and generic or they might be specific to a subject area. TAs are held accountable for the goal setting and parents are expected to participate. Hunter reports that the TA system gives the teaching staff opportunities to integrate by encouraging conversation between and among teachers. He expects that TAs know what is happening for each member of their TA group in each of their classes. Although it may seem contrived, TAs answering to parents about subject area concerns forces the teachers to communicate with one another regarding the academic progress of students in their TA groups. Communication such as this removes some of the isolation associated with teaching and allows teachers to grow in community themselves.

Hunter ensures that each subject area has a subject dean who serves as coordinator for teachers in that subject area. Subject-area teachers are expected to educate their colleagues about their discipline through professional development presentations throughout the year. The math department, for example, will do a presentation that is a brief overview of the concepts that TAs need to be aware of so that they can advise, consult and facilitate their TA group students and their parents from an informed perspective. If the TA is unable to satisfy the needs of the parents for information in a particular discipline, they set up an interview time with the specific teacher for the parent. Hunter reports that every situation is different and is handled on an individual basis, depending on the needs of the student and the parent. The type of service offered is determined on a case-by-case basis, but the general parameters are to have parents interact directly with the TA and not the other teachers.

Planning for the Next Crop

In June when lists of the new students from the feeder schools arrive, the TAs contact every new student and new parent. Interviews with these students are scheduled for evenings in the second week in June and prior to the beginning of second semester. During these interviews, the TA is expected to explain the two-day rotating program the school uses to schedule classes, and to give handout sheets that explain all the TA's responsibilities. Everything is explained so that the parents know what the TA is supposed to be doing. This adds another level of accountability to TAs. The TAs also outline the school's expectations of the parents. Descriptors of how the TA system works are distributed so that parents and students have a chance to familiarize themselves with the program before they begin.

Hunter has learned that to run the TA program effectively, sufficient time has to be provided. In a traditional school setting, such as the one at St. Lawrence, the TA time has to come from other instructional time. The staff struggles with how to keep the TA time effective and relevant without penalizing other areas. In Hunter's words, the TA program gives teachers "a pretty onerous responsibility...especially in our structure." Staff members provide activities that allow students to see a particular purpose. They have to give time where students are able to get to know the teacher advisor on a one-to-one basis because establishing a level of trust between TAs and group members is important. Hunter believes that this trust builds confidence and allows for more open sharing of information. Students recognize that the TA is there to guide them throughout their high school career and beyond. Without trust and confidence in each other the task would be difficult.

How does your garden grow?

Hunter describes the advisory role of teachers and the college system as a focus for professional development and administrative leadership within the building. Both these concepts contribute to the uniqueness of the school as a place that nurtures students as they learn—the way plants are nurtured in a garden. The philosophy that has TA's holding students to account also underlies the treatment of staff. Hunter reports that teachers meet with a member of the administrative team once a month. At these monthly meetings teachers and administrators talk about teacher growth plans. Instead of having one meeting at the beginning of the year and one meeting at the end, which is the more usual arrangement, the staff at St. Lawrence has set up monthly reviews of the goals in the teacher growth plans. The agenda includes more than that. Hunter explains about the meetings:

> So we talk about that (teacher growth plans). We talk about
> any attendance issues that come up with students. We talk

*about any academic issues that come up with students, and
from there we can determine if the issue should stay with
the TAs plan, or does it need to have a counsellor's referral,
does it need to have an administration referral, and what
is that relationship with parents. What plan are we on? Are
we at a corrective stage? Are we at a consequential stage?
Where are we at?*

The staff have a lot of dialogue around what they can do to support and facilitate teacher advisor groups, and they are held to account in the monthly meetings with the administration. These meetings seem to provide an opportunity for conversation with administrative team members who then have an opportunity to negotiate with teachers the circumstances, significance and expectations for changes in the school.

Hunter describes that in his experience in the self-paced setting, the TA function is more defined and there is an opportunity throughout the day for TAs who are not teaching other classes, and for students who are not attending other classes, to communicate in a less structured way. Giving the teacher the additional responsibility normally found in a self-paced setting where little time is devoted to these responsibilities is perceived by Hunter as more difficult. The St. Lawrence customized TA model fits this particular situation, and allows teachers and students the time to interact in meaningful ways in the TA program while expecting students and teachers to carry out the rest of their day in a normal class schedule. It is a hybrid of the traditional high school and a school with completely individualized programs.

Blooms and Second Harvest

The outcome-based model with its opportunity for reassessment contributes to increased student performance, according to Hunter. He reports that each assignment and test is marked on a standard using a rubric. There are basically two standards. The minimum pass, a subset of the pillar advocating complete education, is a 65 percent. "What we say to students is before you progress to the next academic level in whatever subject area you are taking you have to have a minimum grade of 65 percent," explains Hunter, "so we use that as a bit of a bench mark." He believes that the 65 percent minimum for promotion to the next level is a contributing factor to his students achieving the acceptable standard on their standardized achievement scores. Students who are at a school awarded 54 or 55 are strongly encouraged, through the TA program, to take the extra steps (reassessment) to get to the 65 percent minimum. The aim is to reach mastery (80 percent) through reassessment. The result of this approach is that the minimum pass is 65 percent, not 50 percent. Mastery requires a score of 80 percent, which indicates that the student has demonstrated knowledge of all the concepts in an acceptable manner or beyond an acceptable manner. If the student has a 55 percent in an assignment, whether it is a written assignment or an oral presentation, a quiz, or a test of any type, he or she is allowed to reassess, that is do the assignment again.

It is the TA who makes the call on whether or not and when a student is prepared for a reassessment. Hunter explains that the student meets with the subject teacher. Together they look at activities that the student has to complete in order to demonstrate that the materials have been reviewed to the extent where the reassessment shows improvement. The TA is involved in that loop and reports to the subject teacher that the student has done the required review materials and is ready for a reassessment. The student is then sent to the study centre, where a member of the support staff holds the reassessment test and activity bank that the teacher has established and developed while planning for the course.

When the reassessment is graded, two possible grades are considered; a 65 percent or an 80 percent. If the student demonstrates the acquisition of the skills and concepts related to that particular assessment with a minimum pass, they receive a 65 percent. Hunter gives an example,

> If they are in English 10 and they are getting 55 but they reassess and through reassessment the teacher says "Yes, this work is good." It is not mastery level. There are still a few things he needs to work on but it is at least a 65 percent. That is what they will give them. Then the student works towards the next assessment activity in the same way.

Hunter says that he and his staff call their approach "setting the student up for success". They believe that when the student sees the mark, it motivates him or her even more to complete assignments and assessment activities. Students learn that even if they do not do well on an activity, as long as they are willing to do review work and demonstrate that they have completed the review material, they have an opportunity to better their results. Students enter exams with the mind-set that they are there to do their best, and because they have been able to establish that minimum pass students feel confident about the subject or unit of study on the exam. Hunter reports that he firmly believes that the minimum pass and a chance for reassessment are both factors that contribute to good results on standardized test scores as well as school-awarded marks. Opportunities for plants to re-establish themselves and to grow toward what nurtures them are factors in the success of the garden.

Increasing Yield

Hunter is proud to report that the science department performs well on the standardized tests. One of the reasons Hunter gives for this success is the focus for curriculum delivery in that department: hands-on programming. Hunter explains that everything is basically experiential with the students. The number of field trips has increased. Student are gathering data, recording information in real time, and not just doing it on the computer or from texts. Hunter says proudly, "They are actually engaged in something they have to do with their hands. We find that our students work best that way in this area. I think that is evident in our achievement results."

Another reason for the success in science reported by Hunter is that science teachers at St. Lawrence teach all science courses. Math teachers teach all math courses as well. "I do not have a teacher that teaches physics 30 and that's it. That teacher will teach Science 10 or Science 24 or Science 14," he explains. Once teachers have been in the school for four or five years, they are expected to have taught almost the entire curriculum for their subject area so that they establish a good understanding of what the students need to know at every grade level.

However, according to Hunter and the other sources, even in Science, St. Lawrence students do not score in the excellence range in significant numbers. Moving students into the excellence range has become a goal for many of the curriculum areas. The goal is to get the number closer to the percentage of students in the province who meet the standard for excellence. School-based marks are on par with the provincial averages but the overall marks are still lower. School marks are combined with exam marks and averaged. Because the exam marks are below provincial average, they pull the final blended marks down.

This unwillingness to remain satisfied with improvements to date seems to provide evidence of Hunter's commitment to continuous improvement. As Gardener, he is always searching for ways to improve yield and quality. Although the Mastery approach has had a positive effect on the school-awarded portion of the final marks, the provincial exam portion of the marks are still below provincial average. This indicates a need to focus on this area in order to attain the next goal of more students achieving the standard of excellence.

A Market for the Produce

About four years ago St. Lawrence initiated a program that employed a full-time career practitioner on staff. This individual works with the students and the Teacher Advisors in areas of career planning and initiates visits to the school by university and other post-secondary vocational and technical institutes to present information about programs. Businesses visit the school or send representatives to encourage career choices. This focus on career capitalizes on the real-life expectations of students to be employed at the end of high school if not sooner. By providing the positive vision of a prosperous future through the introduction of the career programs, the school and staff motivate students who might otherwise be discouraged by gloomy prospects of an unemployed or under-employed future. The seeds of hope planted by the career practitioner act as a catalyst—or fertilizer—to encourage growth and learning at the school.

Another advantage of the TA system reported by Hunter is that students are counselled into the courses that are appropriate for their abilities and their career choices. Time and professional effort ensure a better fit for the program to the student. "Sometimes people call that streaming but it is not streaming from the perspective of streaming the student," explains Hunter. Prerequisite skills and concepts are required for a student to be eligible to continue in a stream. TAs assess the students' readiness for a particular program and determine whether or not they have acquired skills and concepts. "We always provide opportunities for students to demonstrate that they can go back into the academic stream." According to Hunter, moving from a non-academic to an academic course happens at any grade level at St. Lawrence. "They can do that in grade 10, they can do that in grade 11 or they can go into the non-academic stream right throughout in grade 12, when we feel they have some good groundwork in some concept areas." Hunter is proud of this flexibility. TAs work with students to help them decide where their strengths are. Students not proficient in math are steered towards a Science 30 or a Biology 30. These science courses depend more heavily on English than mathematics. Students who are stronger in math are steered towards the Physics 30 and Chemistry 30 courses, which have more emphasis on math. The focus is not on how the school performs on the standardized tests, but on individual success. Teachers actually resist the averaging of test scores. The improvement of individuals leads logically to improved average results. No door is ever closed to a student at St. Lawrence. Like plants in a garden that are receiving too much or too little shade, these students are relocated to ensure that they reach their full potential, their full bloom. When each plant in the garden improves, the whole garden improves.

In order for students to stay in the academic stream they are expected to maintain the 65 percent average. "If you maintain a 65 you go to the next level. If you cannot, we put you on a probationary timeline." Students make changes at the end of October. They are permitted and encouraged to move either way. Hunter explains that the TA might say, "Okay you can be in the academic stream because you demonstrated through activities that you were able to maintain mastery in some and a minimum pass in others." Throughout the semester, if it appears that the student is unable to maintain the 65 percent average, they remain in a non-academic stream.

The philosophy reported by Hunter is that if everyone is working together no student will slip through the cracks, although the truth is that sometimes students do. "It is all an issue of time," says Hunter. "We grapple with the question do we need more time for advisory (TA) or do we need less time? Or do we change how our time allotments are structured within our schedule?" Hunter admits that scheduling, and even staffing, influences the way that students are successful. Scheduling and staffing aside, what remains clear is the commitment to each individual student and his or her academic success. It appears that he flattened the line between responsibility and behaviour through what he reports as his continuous appreciation of the work that teachers do and of each of them as individuals. He is quick to acknowledge the work of his staff. His care and concern for people in general is evident in his relaxed, caring demeanour and his high expectations for himself and others. His motives appear to be genuine. He wants learning and growth opportunities for students and staff, here in his Garden, St. Lawrence High School.

The Gardeners

Encouraging teachers to expand their repertoire is a leadership practice that seems to promote and permit academic success. Planning professional development around a theme is another leadership practice identified by Hunter as contributing to the success of students and teachers. He explains, "This year we are focusing on Differentiating Instruction (DI). We have not started anything on it yet, but we are looking into setting up some speakers." Teachers are provided with literature to read so that they can become familiar with the concepts of DI. Hunter has communicated to them that staff meeting time periods devoted to professional development will focus on discussing and incorporating learning modalities. The idea is not to just talk about DI but to experience differentiated strategies as a learner. At their administrator's meeting, Hunter suggested that the team use a survey for teachers on DI to help them understand about their own learning styles. He sees as his direct responsibility the job of keeping the staff informed and keeping them current with professional materials so they can be held responsible for the jobs they are doing in the classroom.

Hunter uses the conversations with staff to move them from the event, the emphasis on DI, to a sense of responsibility. This, in turn, leads them to a change in behaviour that is more sensitive to DI. Hunter seems to be firmly in charge and vicariously responsible for the education of the students in the school through his teachers. His sense of responsibility to them shows through in his conversation and through his school newsletters and other documents posted on the website.

Teachers are encouraged to participate in the planning and implementation of the professional development initiatives. "The way we set up our meetings here, I believe facilitates the type of dialogue we want." He reports that staff meetings involve the large group. Whenever the teachers want to break into a smaller grouping, they use their college group. A college meeting is a heterogeneous grouping of everybody, where they talk about issues. Flip chart sheets are used to record the ideas. "We have sheets all over the place when we are discussing some things that we need to change." The staff is revisiting the operational plans that have been in place for five years. They are having that discussion at a college meeting. If there is a need to break that down further into smaller groups, then the staff divides further into subject area groups. Support staff is included, caretakers, teaching assistants, everybody is a member of a college. This ensures that feedback is gathered from everyone. Through this structure Hunter demonstrates how feedback and input were valued and expected at St. Lawrence. He is demonstrating his understanding of how everything in a garden contributes to the overall health of plants. Promoting interaction in large, small and even smaller groups, encourages participation and inclusion.

Maximum Yield

Hunter identifies his own leadership style as collaborative. He thinks it is important to be collaborative in the educational climate he is creating. He believes there needs to be a level of shared decision making. He has three vice-principals in the school. He shares responsibilities for running the school with them and does not take those delegated tasks back. "I allow them to work with those responsibilities full circle. We set our structure up that way so that certain teachers, and students, and counsellors will deal with the same administrator." Hunter is responsible for one of the four colleges. When he does teacher-growth plans he does them with the people in his grouping, and the other three vice-principals do the same with the group of teachers from their assigned college. Through the structure, he puts the administrator or person who is responsible for holding teachers to account, in close proximity to the teachers, which adds to the credibility and the significance of the administrator. The accountability conversations are held between the teacher and their college administrator, who is someone they work closely with. Approval from this person might be of greater significance to the teacher because of the proximity or the relationship. Risks of non-compliance are better understood, and impacts of past circumstances are more likely to be known to staff within the college structure.

Hunter and his administrative team use the inquiry process when they are providing opportunities for dialogue with teachers. They believe that the inquiry approach brings out the reflective practitioner in the staff. The objective is to have staff think about what has happened and how it might have turned out differently. Teachers are encouraged to think about the aspects that they would like to continue to use in their practice of teaching and the things they might want to change. Teachers interact in colleges, in subject groups and as a complete staff as they consider important questions of policy and practice.

Hunter reveals that building the leadership capacity of the school is also important to him. There are subject deans who coordinate teachers in the subject areas, and there are college deans who head up the respective colleges. Deans run the college meetings.

Administrators attend as one of the group. They provide feedback and an administrative perspective. Information from a college meeting is brought back to the administrative team comprised of the principal and vice-principals and then to the larger administrative team that includes all of the deans. The extended administrative team is comprised of about 15 people; four administrators and the coordinating teachers or deans. They make decisions based on the feedback from everyone.

College deans are selected through an interview process. The role is one of leadership in the administration of the school, dealing with professional development issues, with student academic issues, and with program issues that are generic in nature. Subject deans have a specific program requirement or program need, but when it comes to the college, the college dean considers issues through a broader lens. If other subject areas are affected, the college dean instigates the dialogue at the college level or he or she comes back to administration and suggests that the concern is not a college meeting topic because it is just a math concern or a math and science concern. If a majority of subject area deans show an interest in pursuing a dialogue or a topic further, then the college dean facilitates further investigation.

The system as described by Hunter sounds very straight forward and inclusive. One wonders if the staff understand how the system works as well as he does. Staff may be less aware of the purpose of the structure than the leaders in their building. Often staff have never really thought about it, or perhaps they accept it as 'the way we do things around here'. Teachers may feel that meetings are a waste of time. Perhaps Hunter has convinced his staff otherwise.

The meeting structure seems to allow for the kind of inclusion Hunter describes. All meetings occur once a month—staff meetings, deans' meetings, college, and subject area meetings. Hunter explains, "If we can fit in two meetings a month, depending upon our calendar, then we will repeat the subject meeting." There are also committee meetings such as awards committees, graduation committee, student council, and the technology committee that meet from time to time. A program has been established where lead technology teachers provide professional development sessions in their subject area and college area. Sharing expertise is something that Hunter reports as an important expectation of teachers. As they share expertise, so too will they share in decision making and responsibility.

The consistency with which people in the building are treated is obvious. Everyone is honoured for their contribution and is supported in their learning. The key to it all is a structure that allows and encourages relationships that nourish and challenges each individual to develop. Whether student or teacher, support staff or administrative team, everyone grows under the watchful eye of the Gardener.

When things go reasonably right, the plants mature, gain strength and robustness as they ripen into the reaping season, whether the reaping is for the beholder's eye or the consumer's stomach. Ultimately there is a harvest and the dried golden remains disintegrate, enriching the soil from which they emerged for the next generation. The gardens and their plots will lie fallow for a season before the Gardener joins the cycle again to practise the art of leavening creation.

Characteristics of a Gardener:
- Nurturing
- Consistent
- Confident
- Courageous
- Curious
- Caring
- Structured

To be effective a Gardener leader needs to:
- Maintain clarity of purpose
- Preserve autonomy for self and others
- Seek contexts where change takes place in a longer-term perspective
- Manage expectations of short-term results
- Be supported

To work with a Gardener Leader, others need to:
- Be patient
- Know that the Gardener will take time to reach sustainable collaborative decisions
- Be prepared to see people "weeded out"

Chapter 7: A Call to Action

Planned or unplanned, sudden or occurring over a longer time, expected or not, change happens. The general perspective is that change, in all aspects of our lives, appears to be accelerating and is happening all the time. Often we make the decision or take the action that is the change. More often, it seems, we are the objects of change.

Whether we are objects of change or participative subjects, some kind of internal adaptation and external adjustment are required for us to re-establish our orientation and a sense of stability in our life. Experienced as a chaotic transition from our current situation to something not quite so certain in the fog of the future, the internal adaptation process is usually the most difficult to navigate, causing distress and disruption for ourselves and those around us.

In making this distinction between change, which can happen in a micro-second, and the human adaptation to change, which inevitably happens over a longer period of time, we want to underline the critical organizational competency of managing transitions. Mandated change, i.e., change over which we have little or no control, is an anxiety-provoking proposition. The journey of getting from here to there can be one of considerable stress, and may result in a natural reaction to conserve the status quo. This is well documented in the annals of psychology and organization behaviour. Effective organizational leadership, particularly in the face of mandated change, requires the competency and considerable skills of managing transitions.

Specifically managing transitions involves the art of motivating and supporting individuals, groups, and organizations in their efforts to move from their present situation, often rooted and oriented in the past, to a more or less well defined place in the future. The journey is often a wandering in the desert of some chaos and confusion where performance and results drop dramatically in the heat of transition before new gains are made in the "promised land". The path a specific transition will take depends on the infinite variety of contexts in which change occurs as well as the limitless mix of characters and characteristics that make for a particular organization.

These five principals have approached the management of transition in different ways given certain context and particular people. The Impresario is a man of energy and enthusiasm: a gregarious, charismatic and highly visible individual who is constantly challenging his followers with new ideas. While his environment is filled with excitement and anticipation, his followers must be prepared to take on the many different challenges thrown their way.

In contrast, the Sherpa works quietly, seemingly in the wings, supporting transition by shouldering tasks and creating a new, stable environment that allows his followers to be focused on teaching for the desired results. Dedicated, selfless and efficient, the Sherpa needs to be aware of when delegation is appropriate and possible, and when his followers need to take responsibility for completing their work and not take his helping nature for granted.

The Coach is the most goal-oriented of these principals, approaching his task of organization transition with a steady, analytical calm. His followers work best when they are open to being coached for performance, and have a clear and realistic approach to setting and meeting their own goals.

PRINCIPAL PORTRAITS
WHO THEY ARE AND HOW TO WORK WITH THEM

	The Impresario	The Sherpa
Characteristics	• Charismatic • Visible • Honest • Transparent • Sharing • Commanding • Fun • Respected	• Dedicated • Harmonious • Efficient • Selfless • Detailed • Individualist • Sacrificing • Invisible
To be Effective this leader needs to ...	• Acknowledge others • Keep an open forum for expression • Create opportunities in a new and exciting environments • Seek efficiencies • Ensure people are in roles where they can thrive	• Manage time well • Be organized and structured • Prioritize carefully • Seek ways to streamline work processes and paperwork • Delegate tasks as appropriate
To work with this leader others need to...	• Be prepared to take the good with the bad • Be open to "going for the ride" on many potential opportunities • Be prepared to work independently and to a high standard • Put students first	• Take responsibility for completing their work • Acknowledge the "heavy lifting" of others • Manage expectations • Support where possible

The Coach	The Rescuer	The Gardener
• Goal oriented • Informal • Focused • Mature • Aware • Team-focused • Steady • Calm	• Courageous • Supporting • Modeling • Humble • Strong-willed • Empathetic • Trusting • Trustworthy	• Nurturing • Consistent • Confident • Courageous • Accountable • Curious • Caring • Structured
• Accept the role as a leader who works through others • Identify work that is both strategic and uniquely his or hers • Delegate • Recruit staff with complementary skills • Spend time mentoring others	• Seek a challenge • Seek new and novel contexts • Create pressure for change • Seek opportunities for innovation • Work with people he or she can respect	• Maintain clarity of purpose • Preserve autonomy for self and others • Seek contexts where change takes place in a longer term perspective • Manage expectations of short term results • Be supported
• Be open to coaching for performance • Be willing to acknowledge performance gaps and opportunities • Be able to set realistic goals to close performance gaps and exploit opportunities	• Be open to change and innovation • Be ready to go with the flow • Work for improvement • Recognize if they are seen as an obstacle to change	• Be patient • Know that the Gardener will take time to reach sustainable collaborative decisions • Be prepared to see people "weeded out" • Enjoy the slow steady progress

The Rescuer has the courage and strong will to take on the new mandates. The challenge for the Rescuer is to create the motivation for change where none apparently exists. Followers will thrive if they are open to change and innovation. They will be supported in their transitions by a leader who is empathetic with the stress felt by people experiencing transition.

The nurturing Gardener has a long-term perspective and will take time to decide on changes that will have a long-lasting impact. Pursuing the goal consistently, the Gardener is not afraid to make the tough decisions and will "weed out" those who are obstacles to a smoother transition. The staff who share the long-term view and maintain clarity of purpose will benefit from the healthy and positive environment the Gardener can provide.

The chart "Principal Portraits: Who they are and how to work with them" provides a summary of the characteristics of these five principals. The chart also gives some insight into what these leaders need to work effectively and what their followers need to know to work effectively with them.

Paths to Results

The Impresario was able to talk to his staff about the audience, the students, who they were really serving. He was clear in his conversation about who came first and what the show was all about. His focus in every conversation about the students and what is best for them succeeded in shifting teachers away from the curriculum and toward the needs of individual students. As a result, students felt more empowered and were encouraged to go to class and learn rather than play cards in the cafeteria. Time in front of the teacher was increased and, by extension, familiarity with the curriculum translated to higher test scores. The Impresario also changed his audience by inviting students with more of an interest in academics to become part of his school population. That, no doubt, also had an effect on the scores. Putting the right person in the right staff role was something else that the Impresario did. From his office, he chose carefully to match the appropriate teachers with different kinds of students, to encourage learning and further impact results.

The Sherpa worked tirelessly to unburden others. He came to the school on weekends to fix furniture, to reinstall programs on computers, to pick up litter, anything that needed doing to make the lives of teachers and students more pleasant and easier. He made his presence known in the hallways on supervision. If there were students in the building, he was among them in his quiet, unassuming way. He believed it was very important to tackle the mounds of paperwork on his own after the students went home. He took on paperwork that teachers might do, freeing the teachers to concentrate on teaching. He continually analyzed and researched ways to improve test scores, and when his research showed a need for cross curricular knowledge he began to move teachers toward generalized assignments and away from grade specific assignments in their subject areas. Putting his expertise to work with a recalcitrant staff was courageous and difficult; however, strengthened by research and resolve, he did the heavy lifting that got the transition underway.

The Coach worked to ensure that the staff of his small school had experiences with other subject-matter teachers at the provincial level. He encouraged and made it possible for them to learn from teachers in other jurisdictions by providing opportunities to mark provincial exams and to pilot new programs. His emphasis on the test score performance, as well as the time he spent analysing and blueprinting for better results, demonstrated to staff and students the importance of the scores as a measure of performance. He paid attention to performance and so *they* paid attention to performance. And this made a difference in performance. Study groups and exam preparation were taken seriously and marks improved as a result.

The Rescuer inherited a school that had hit a low spot. He entered the organization and took command of the crisis. Changes in staff and the development of a caring, safe environment made preparing for exams easier and a focus on academics possible. He was able to recalibrate the school, to shift attention away from strife and chaos toward the job at hand—the education of students. Teachers who were feeling less threatened did a better job with students in the classroom, which resulted in better results from those students. Students were also more relaxed and better able to study. The Rescuer has the ability to stand back and survey the situation, assessing the abilities of those rescued to carry on without him as he contemplates his next move.

The Gardener had the luxury of time to set up a new school and to structure it to maximize growth and learning. Again by researching what might work best, he was able to apply this research by creating a Teacher Advisory system and making the structural adjustment that resulted in the highly successful colleges within the school. From his office, he insisted on each student having one adult they could go to and trust, and he structured his "garden" to accomplish that. He felt strongly that nurturing individual learning would give every student a chance to bloom, to be successful. For this reason the Gardener moved toward a mastery learning structure for the school. Many of his decisions had a direct influence on classrooms and teachers and their sense of responsibility. Subject-area generalists became entirely familiar with all facets of a curriculum, an asset that the Gardener specifically cultivated in his staff. Well trained teacher/mentors made it almost impossible for anyone to slip through the cracks. He modeled what he expected of his staff with his own genuine concern for people. Teachers observed his actions and they learned. His care and attention became their care and attention. For the Gardener, the harvest of this investment in time and attention was the increased scores for his students.

Your First Step

Now you have read the portraits. What could you do next? What call to the future excites you? What small step can you take that will start the journey of a thousand steps? Invite others on staff to join you. Here are some of our well tested suggestions to get you started

1. Generate a list of criteria for developing a school that best matches the educational needs of students, their communities and their societies.

2. Connect with other principals to share their impressions of the archetypes presented in this book. Create a group of likeminded colleagues. Meet regularly to share stories and support one another.

3. Create a list of measureable outcomes that define the success of your school.

4. Imagine the future for your school. Create a compelling vision of the future. Draw it, describe it.

5. Explore different ways of communicating with your staff, students and community to motivate and support them in transitions to the future. What would you need to say to reassure the different stakeholders and have them accept responsibility for moving to the future you have envisioned?

6. Do something that scares you. Take a calculated risk in getting a journey to a new future underway.

7. Dream up other ways you can be successful at leading transitions. Imagine! What are the key metaphors that can inspire and motivate others to follow your lead?

8. List how things would be different in your school if you had total and absolute authority to make the changes that will help your school get to the future.

9. Decide on the strategies and tactics you will employ to ensure coordination and cooperation in your organization as you undergo transition. How will you manage the inevitable potential for conflict or actual conflict?

And in the end...

This book is an invitation for a continuing dialogue. Here at PULSE, it is important to us that you keep in touch. Not enough portraits of principals have been captured for us to study and learn from. If you know of a good principal story, or could suggest a principal that others could emulate, please let us know so we can follow up and keep this story going. Over the years I have interviewed more than 30 principals in different situations. There are always great lessons to be learned, not the least of which is that different people handle different situations differently—and that's okay. Send us your responses and your portraits so we can work with you to publish them for others.

In this book we have introduced you to a number of principals in a number of different contexts and shared their stories of how they managed the transition that resulted from mandated change. We pulled lessons from these portrayals and invited you to do the same. Now we have asked you to join us as we work toward sharing more such stories. We appreciate the time you took from your busy schedule to look at these portraits and to see them from your perspective or frame. We hope you enjoyed the read.

Dr. Nancy Love,
Mel Blitzer,
Marjorie Munroe.
www.pulseinstitute.com

Epilogue: The Voice of a Principal

Typical Example—I got a letter from a kid who probably has not experienced too much success in his life. He is one of my black students. We are a very ethnic community here. Very heterogeneous, the flags on our main street represent all of our different cultures that are here in the building. So Kevin writes me a letter. He is not doing well academically. And he is not doing well attendance-wise. But he has got some skills and abilities in basketball. So rather than just responding to this letter and saying to Kevin, okay fine, I will give you an opportunity even though you have not met all of our criteria to play athletics.

We placed him on a contract that included his teacher advisor, his parents and his coach, and college Vice Principal, and I was just involved in this initial conference to say this is what we are going to do. We are going to hold you to some of the statements you make in there. He makes a statement to say that this is important in his life and he wants it as a motivating factor for him and he wants to be successful in his school studies. So we set him up for that. So we created a daytimer for him where it is his responsibility at the end of every week to go to his teacher; the teacher outlines what he has done. We have given him a minimum number of unexcused absences, which is one. We have given him a minimum number of lates, unexcused, which is five over the course of a week. And we have said no assignments incomplete. Every assignment is complete. It might not be a 65. It might not be a 50, but it is complete. Because if you hand it in, you find out what you have not done well you have got an opportunity to reassess. If you can accomplish those things, your coach will get a green light to say Kevin plays at your discretion. But if you get a red light you sit out for that entire week. You become a passive member of the team rather than an active member of the team. When that happens, then the message for you is to say I need to get my act together for the following week so that I make sure that my report is much more positive and then I can shoot for the next week to play.

So that is setting the kid up for success. That is an example of how we establish a plan for a corrective measure. And we engage everybody in the process. The TA has got a responsibility; the college VP has a responsibility. The kid has a greater responsibility. The parents hook into this and because I am involved in the process every now and then I will just say, like if I am watching the game and I see him sitting, I will come up to him and say why are you sitting? And he will tell me, I screwed up on the course and coach asked me to just kind of think about this. Or I am passive today. So those are the kind of things that we tend to do. I believe that that type of dialogue, that type of collaboration, sets students up for success. When they get to the point where they are in the position of demonstrating they know they are going to try to do the best that they can. To a certain extent those subjective, intangible kinds of elements contribute to scores on achievement tests.

Matthew Hunter, Gardener

Acknowledgements

We would like to thank our reviewers and principals everywhere. They are the unsung heroes of our society. We would especially like to thank the Impresario, the Sherpa, the Coach, the Rescuer and the Gardener.

About the Authors

Dr. Nancy Love, PhD. is the Founder and President of The PULSE Institute. Dr. Love is a workplace effectiveness consultant and an international trainer in workplace mediation and leadership who is dedicated to building leadership capacity and creating world peace—one conversation at a time. She has worked with many organizations to assist them with in-house programs and policy development. Her discovery and development of the PULSE Frame for conversations for change evolved from a lifelong dedication to learning, leadership, accountability and change.

Nancy has a Bachelor of Education in French and Social Studies and a Masters of Education in Administration from the University of Alberta. She received a Doctorate in Educational Research with a specialty in Leadership at the University of Calgary. A former High school principal, annual instructor at the University of Lethbridge Summer Leadership Institute and the author of *Principal Portraits* (2001 and 2004), her interest in and research on the practices of high school principals in a climate of accountability lead her to write a dissertation entitled "Accountability and Change" (2006).

Mel Blitzer is an organization effectiveness leader, business advisor, and educator. His purpose is to partner with leaders, professionals, groups and organizations around the world to assist them in accelerating their dreams, i.e., to achieve great results in pursuit of their business, community and personal goals.

Over the past 25 years, to achieve his purpose, Mel has taken on the roles of director, project manager, management consultant, change agent, educator/trainer, coach and facilitator. As a business advisor and educator Mel has a passion for engaging and challenging people in focused learning experiences. He is adept at guiding leaders, managers and professionals in practical, goal focused processes and programs that lead to improved personal and organizational performance. When there are opportunities to exploit or problems to solve, Mel can offer practical assistance.

Marjorie Munroe is an Associate of The PULSE Institute and a mediator. Her role at PULSE varies. She trains people in the art and the science of effective conversation in a wide variety of contexts across government and industry in the US and Canada. She is Dr. Nancy Love's editor and works with her closely on books and training materials. Marjorie also manages The PULSE Institute website and promotional materials.

Marjorie's passion for training comes from her deeply held belief that the skills mediators use as impartial facilitators of a structured conversation are applicable in a wide variety of contexts: effective speaking and listening as preventative medicine.

Nancy, Mel and Marjorie work together at the PULSE Institute to create and deliver quality workshops, webcasts and keynote addresses on leadership and conflict resolution. They share the firm belief that a structured conversation provides an effective route to managing change. Specific workshops based on the ideas presented in this book are available. We believe in world peace—one conversation at a time.

The PULSE Institute
Suite 640, 1300 8th Street SW
Calgary AB T2R 1B2
www.pulseinstitute.com

Reading List

Accountability in Education: Policy Framework. Edmonton: Alberta Education, 1995.

Coleman, Peter, and Charlotte Nancy Love. *Principal Portraits 2: A Look at Successful Secondary School Leadership and Management Practices in Alberta and British Columbia*. Kelowna: Society for the Advancement of Excellence in Education, 2004.

Lawrence-Lightfoot, Sara. *The Good High School: Portraits of Character and Culture*. Basic Books, 1985.

Love, Charlotte Nancy. *Accountability and Change: Portraits of Five High School Principals*. Calgary, 2006.

—. *Principal Portraits: A Look at Successful Secondary School Leadership and Management Practices in Alberta and British Columbia*. Kelowna: Society for the Advancement of Excellence in Education, 2001.

Wolcott, Harry. *Man in the Principal's Office (revised)*. AltaMira Press, 2003.